Contents

Preface 5

George Ridley's family tree 8

1 The best amateur comic singer 11

2 Balmbra's 23

3 The Gateshead vocalist 32

4 The Tyne Concert Hall 43

5 *On the Road to Brighton* 62

6 *George Ridley's Local Song Book* 76

7 *George Ridley's New Local Song Book* 86

8 *A Choice Collection of Tyneside Songs* 96

9 *Allan's Illustrated Edition of Tyneside Songs* 105

10 Catchy 118

11 'The Geordie National Anthem' 132

12 George Ridley's legacy 143

References 151

Sources 164

Discography 169

Song and Tune Index 172

Name index 175

The procession along Scotswood Road, Newcastle, on 9 June 1962 celebrates the centenary of George Ridley's Blaydon Races. Councillor Leslie Cuthbertson, Newcastle Centenary Committee chairman, doffs his topper as the omnibus passes the Cattle Market.

Preface

Few songs – or, at least, few choruses – are as famous in North East England as George Ridley's *Blaydon Races*, and it is one of few examples of regional culture that are known across Britain, and even beyond. Yet the song was not a great success in George's lifetime, and soon after he died, his younger brother, Stephenson eclipsed him, even on Tyneside, by becoming the Mile Champion of England.

Their parents were a working class couple who had married in Gateshead in 1826. George was their third child and arrived in 1835. Two more children had followed by 1843, when eight-year-old George became a *trapper* in a coal pit, opening and closing ventilation doors. In time, he became a *putter*, pushing tubs of coal from the *hewers* at the face to the bottom of the shaft, and bringing back empty ones. By 1853, he had two sisters and six brothers; and, probably in the later 1850s, he got a surface job, taking wagons of coal down a railway line from the pithead to loading staithes next to the Tyne. One day, he was seriously injured. When he eventually recovered, he was unfit for manual work, but had to earn a living.

The industrial revolution had produced large working class communities on Tyneside, and many young, skilled and comparatively well paid male workers had money to spare for the 'music saloons' and 'concert halls'. George was a talented singer of older Tyneside, Irish and Scottish songs, and by 1861 he was a full-time professional entertainer. He began writing songs about local events and celebrities, and though he took some tunes from 'local', Scots and Irish songs, he used several minstrel tunes from the USA, where a Civil War was raging. The local popularity of his sixteen surviving songs – all but three of those we know he wrote –

tells tell us a good deal about Tyneside social conditions, and also about workers' attitudes to the police, bosses' lackeys and professional sportsmen.

There was considerable capital investment in some Newcastle venues, which held over two thousand people, and their managers had to provide variety to fill all the seats. John Balmbra's Wheat Sheaf Music Saloon and George Stanley's Tyne Concert Hall were becoming part of national – and international – networks; but Ridley's output of new material was too modest to get regular engagements there, so he worked in Mechanics' Institutes and pubs. Then, in 1864, after a career of less than three years, he died aged 29.

Many of Ridley's lyrics remained in print throughout the late 19th century, thanks to Thomas Allan's songbooks. In 1908, James Cosgrove, 'J.C. Scatter', a Tyneside music hall comedian, recorded *Blaydon Races* on wax cylinders. In 1912, Newcastle-born Charles Ernest Catcheside, a former London-based music hall singer, recorded *Cushie Butterfield* as 'Ernest Warrington'; and it and *Blaydon Races* appeared in J.G. Windows' *Tyneside Songs*, with piano arrangements by 'C.E. Catcheside-Warrington'.

Thanks to North East soldiers and sailors, fans of Newcastle United football club, and others, *Blaydon Races* became famous across Britain and beyond. From the 1950s, it and *Cushie Butterfield* appeared on shellac discs; and after the centenary of *Blaydon Races* in 1962 both appeared on vinyl discs. In 1972, Frank Graham republished *Allan's Illustrated Tyneside Songs*, with its edited versions of some Ridley songs, and in 1973 Graham published my *George Ridley*, which contained his surviving original lyrics. Windows' *Tyneside Songs* remained in print until 1999.

My warm thanks go to Paul Baker and Vicki Gilbert for their hospitality and comradeship. Vin Arthey, Vic Gammon and Keith Gregson read one or more drafts of this book. Vic found the tunes and organised the recording of the songs by himself, Terry Conway, Benny Graham, Johnny Handle, Stewart Hardy, Jim Mageean and Brian Watson. Ray Stephenson, Brian and Helen Mawson, Peter Jefferies and Anni Fentiman supplied valuable information. Anna Flowers of Tyne Bridge Publishing has been supportive, as have colleagues at Gateshead Libraries, Newcastle Library, Tyne & Wear Archives and the National Library of Australia.

The References, Sources, Discography and Indexes are mainly for readers who want to do further research, or to check mine.

Dave Harker
May 2012

'Away we went along Collingwood Street', 9 June 1901. The procession from Balmbra's gets underway.

George Ridley's family tree

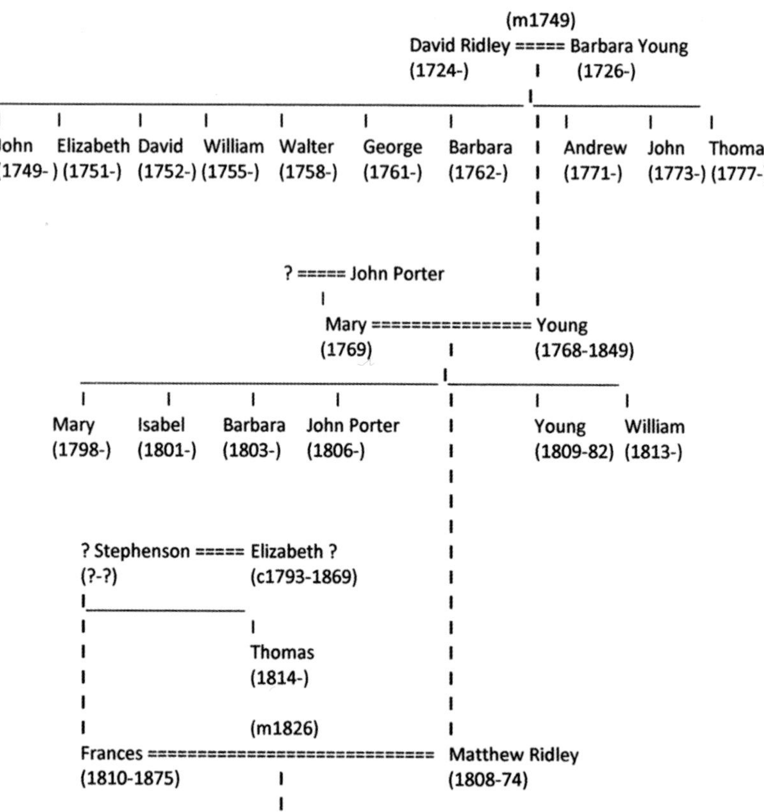

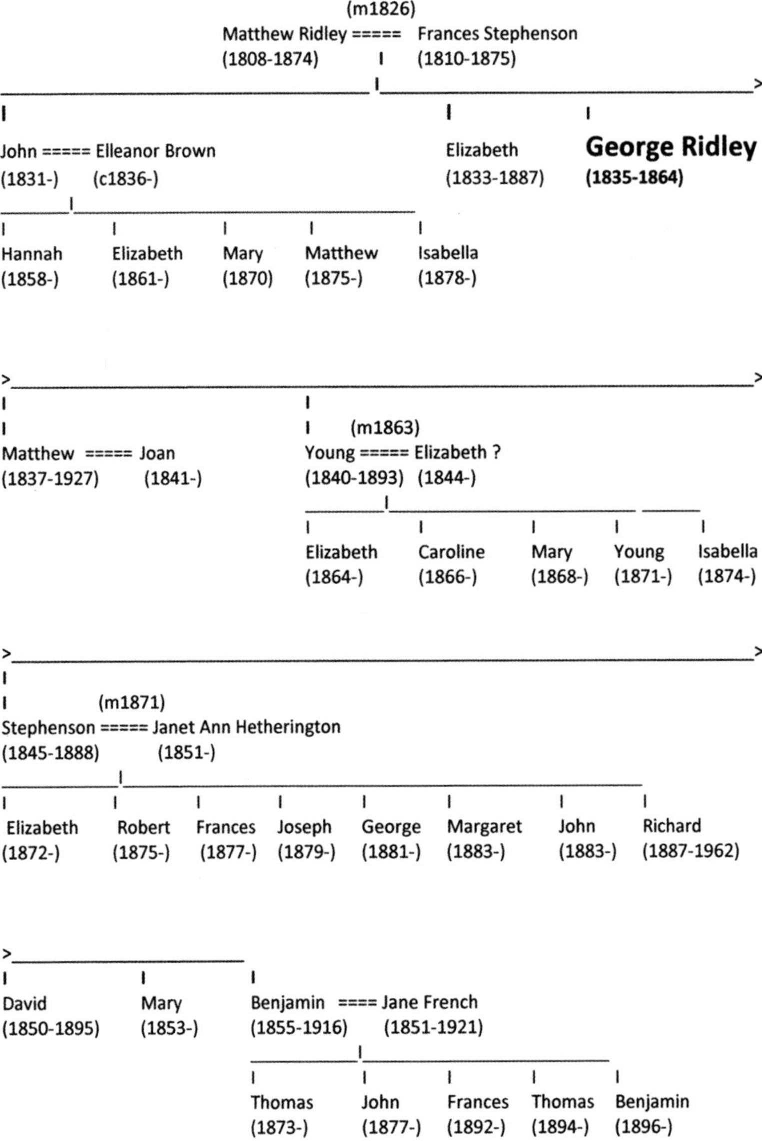
(m1826)
Matthew Ridley ===== Frances Stephenson
(1808-1874) (1810-1875)
John ===== Elleanor Brown
(1831-) (c1836-)
Elizabeth
(1833-1887)
George Ridley
(1835-1864)
Hannah
(1858-)
Elizabeth
(1861-)
Mary
(1870)
Matthew
(1875-)
Isabella
(1878-)
Matthew ===== Joan
(1837-1927) (1841-)
(m1863)
Young ===== Elizabeth ?
(1840-1893) (1844-)
Elizabeth
(1864-)
Caroline
(1866-)
Mary
(1868-)
Young
(1871-)
Isabella
(1874-)
(m1871)
Stephenson ===== Janet Ann Hetherington
(1845-1888) (1851-)
Elizabeth
(1872-)
Robert
(1875-)
Frances
(1877-)
Joseph
(1879-)
George
(1881-)
Margaret
(1883-)
John
(1883-)
Richard
(1887-1962)
David
(1850-1895)
Mary
(1853-)
Benjamin ==== Jane French
(1855-1916) (1851-1921)
Thomas
(1873-)
John
(1877-)
Frances
(1892-)
Thomas
(1894-)
Benjamin
(1896-)

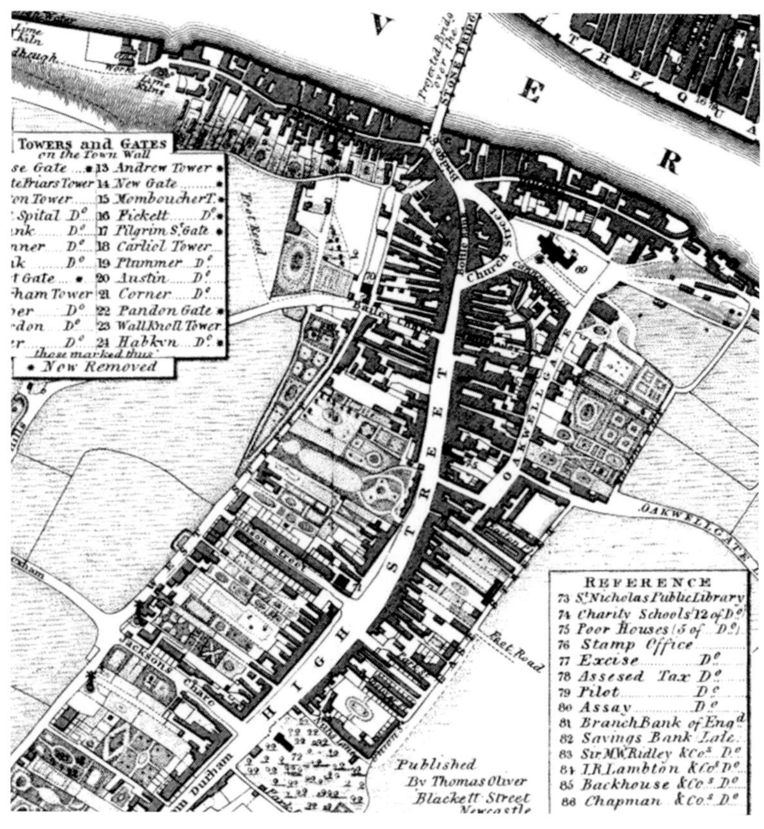

Thomas Oliver, Plan of Newcastle and Gateshead, 1830.

1 The best amateur comic singer

In 1749, 25-year-old David Ridley married Barbara Young, aged 23, in St.Nicholas' Church, Newcastle, and by 1777, they had produced eleven children. Their eighth, Young Ridley, was born in 1768. Probably in the mid-1790s, he married John Porter's daughter, Mary, born in Gateshead in 1769. Young Ridley became a 'Mariner', but between 1798 and 1813 they had seven children. Their fifth child, Matthew, was born in Wrekenton, above Gateshead, around 1808.

By 1811, Gateshead's population was about 9,000 and 11,000 more lived in the Poor Law Union district. By 1821, almost 12,000 were living in the town's 1, 600 houses at an average of eight per dwelling.[1] By 1827, many inhabited the 'very narrow and dirty' Pipewellgate and Hillgate, near the Tyne, or lived in High Street, which was 'one continuous line of buildings of various and irregular appearance' from Sunderland Road to Bottle Bank.[2]

Frances Stephenson had been born in Gateshead around 1810. On 26 September 1830, [3] she married Matthew Ridley in St Mary's Church. They were both 'of the Working Classes'.[4]

By 1831, the town's population was 15,000 ; and in 1832, 93 of the 234 people who died of cholera were from Pipewellgate.[5] John Ridley was born that year and Elizabeth followed in 1833. In 1835, apart from scattered iron works, quarries, collieries, hamlets and gentry's houses, most of the district was agricultural. From the roof of the Moot Hall in Newcastle, St Mary's Church tower dominated the landscape, even on a dark and stormy day.

John Wilson Carmichael, 'A View of Gateshead'.

George Ridley arrived on 10 February 1835,[6] and was baptised in St Mary's on 1 March.[7] Matthew followed in 1837 and Young in 1840.

By 1841, Gateshead's population approached 20,000. The average number in each dwelling was under six, but the density near the Tyne was far higher. The Ridley family lived on the west side of lower High Street. Matthew senior was a rope-maker; but he was given to 'combining that with the occupation of a Pitman', and 'sometimes followed the one and sometimes the other'.[8]

In 1842, Messrs Easton & Company opened Oakwellgate Colliery,[9] a quarter of a mile east of High Street,[10] and Lord Ravensworth received 'Wayleave rents' for the waggonway crossing his land.[11] It was probably at Oakwellgate that Matthew Ridley senior had 'a longish turn at pit work'.[12] *Viewers* – colliery managers – colluded with hard-pressed parents, to send infant boys underground as *trappers*. They crouched in the dark, opening and closing ventilation doors, for twelve hours a day. Adult *hewers* worked shorter shifts. So did teenage *putters*, who pushed trams of coal along rails from the *hewers* to the bottom of the pit shaft.[13]

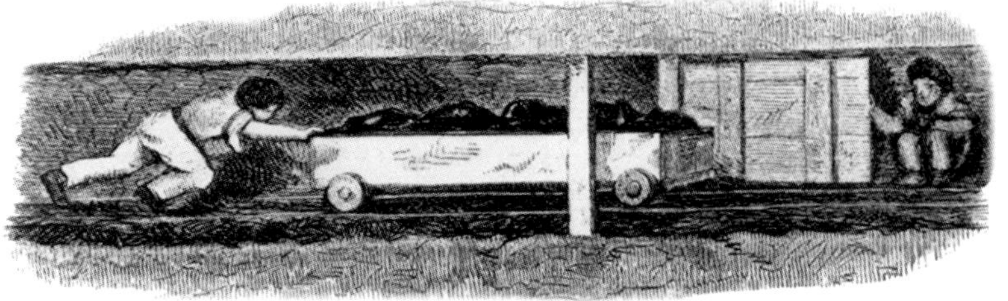

A putter and trapper (The Cyclopaedia of Useful Arts, 1840-1845.

Parliament made it illegal to send boys under the age of ten down mines after 1 March 1843,[14] but Matthew Ridley had 'a large Family to provide for'. Just before that deadline, at 'the early age of 8 years', George was 'sent' to Oakwellgate as a trapper, 'so that his small earnings might be added to the common fund which needed even these small helps'. 'Under these unfavourable circumstances it is easy to see that his education must have been of the simplest'. He may have had little or no formal schooling at all, and he barely learned how to write; but he had only a 'brief stay' at Oakwellgate.[15]

Since its foundation in 1842, the Miners' Association had flourished. Early in April 1844, members in other regions supported a strike by North East pitmen and boys, who wanted to break the *bond*, the contract that tied them to one pit for a year.[16] There were *blacklegs* – strike-breakers – at Oakwellgate Colliery,[17] but late that month the Eastons offered the lease for sale.[18] Elsewhere, Lord Londonderry, a major coal owner, imported 3,500 'foreigners', including many desperately poor people, from his Irish estates, to be *blacklegs* and Londonderry and others paid *candymen* – ruffians – to evict strikers' families from tied cottages.

Strikers and their wives wrote, sang and sold printed copies of songs all over northern England to raise money. By late July, most had given in, but one of Londonderry's pits remained closed through August.[19]

Tyne Main or Friar's Goose Colliery, known locally as the 'Gyuess', was a mile east of Gateshead, near the Tyne, so it was liable to flooding. The High Main Seam was 100 metres down, so Thomas Easton had designed a large steam pump, which drained almost 900 litres of water per stroke, while another pump drained the Low Main Seam, 180 metres down.

University of Newcastle

Thomas Harrison Hair:
Friar's Goose Pumping Station around 1840.

At most pits, safety equipment was rudimentary, maintenance was poor and workers' lives were cheap. The 'Gyeuss' was no exception. In 1843, when 19-year-old Robert Kears ascended the shaft in a *corf* – wicker basket – two men below heard something fall.

> One of them ascended supposing that some stones had fallen down, but finding that not to be the case, descended again, when the deceased was discovered lying dead at the bottom of the shaft. It was supposed he had been thrown out of the corf by its becoming entangled with the 'rapper-rope' [signal cable], which was broken.

In April 1844, during the strike, three *deputies* – safety specialists – had gone down the pit to 'keep the workings in proper condition'. At noon, 'three others descended to relieve them'.

> They had been seated on a rolley, to which an ass was harnessed, when they were buried by a fall of stone from the roof. Five hours elapsed before they were got out; and one of them had to assist in his own liberation, by sawing through a block of stone. Another named William Ridley, was dreadfully crushed, and is scarcely expected to recover. The third — John Caldwell — (a married man with a family) — was killed.[20]

They were 'under Byker Hill on the opposite side of the Tyne'.

It was probably after the strike that George Ridley went to the 'Gyuess'. When he got home he 'used to amuse himself and his companions by cutting out figures in paper' and, 'taking possession of the Rabbit house', he would 'draw a cloth across the front' and 'set his mimic scene in motion'. He 'had a taste for entertaining, and was never better pleased' than 'when amusing his companions by his rich mimicry' and singing.[21]

From 1845, Irish landowners made a terrible famine worse by exporting grain. Many migrants came to Tyneside and some arrived via Scotland. Most from southern and western Ireland settled in Newcastle's All Saints Parish, while most from Ulster lived in Gateshead.[22] On Wednesday 3 January 1849, an Irishman called Denis O'Neil arrived in Gateshead from Canongate in Edinburgh and lodged with William Williams and his family in a back yard in the middle of Pipewellgate. That night, he began 'vomiting and purging' – suffering from diarrhoea – and by Sunday, Williams had 'the choler'. Duncan Matheson found him in a 'hovel under the *nom-de-guerre* of a lodging house', where there were two people in each of the 24 beds. The 'wretchedness and misery' was 'beyond description'. Within a week, a woman died of cholera 'in great agony', and a man died soon after.[23] Pipewellgate was still dirty and overcrowded.

The cholera spread to Hillgate, and 'the most densely populated and filthiest parts of the borough', but householders near the Workhouse objected to it being a 'refuge' for the sick.[24] By the 23rd, eighteen had died in Pipewellgate's 156 houses. By the end of the year, 110 out of the 186 people who died of cholera breathed their last in Pipewellgate.[25]

Gateshead Libraries

East entrance to Pipewellgate, 1844.

Young Ridley, Matthew's father, died in summer in High Street, probably of natural causes, since he was 81.

By 1851, 25,000 or so Gateshead people lived in 3,379 houses, at an average of almost eight per dwelling. Most still lived near the Tyne, including 71 in one house in Hillgate, and there were many more such dwellings in Pipewellgate. The railway line from York and London now crossed the Tyne via the High Level Bridge, industry had developed, and rows of new and airy streets ran west off upper High Street.

Elizabeth Stephenson, Frances Ridley's 58-year-old mother, lived in High Street. She was a 'Pauper', but her 37-year-old son, Thomas, was a 'Bricklayer'. Frances and Matthew Ridley lived in Pollock's Yard, off lower High Street. Sixteen-year-old George was a 'Coal Miner', 14-year-old Matthew was a 'Hatter', 11-year-old Young was apprenticed to a 'Hatter', six-year-old Stephenson was a 'Scholar' and baby David was one. Twenty-year-old John had left home, as had 18-year-old Elizabeth, who was a domestic servant for William Harvey, a general merchant, in Westgate, Newcastle.

For over a decade, around 300 Gateshead people had died each year, 'owing to the artificial aggravation of natural diseases'. The Local Board of Health began work, but some of its members owned 'very ill-conditioned house property in the borough'. In 1853, single families occupied 1,838 dwellings, while 3,660 squeezed into 1,585. Only 64 houses had water closets and only 80 or so had 'faecal drainage'. Four-fifths of the population lived in poor districts and at least half were in dwellings that were unfit for human habitation. Well over 2,000 people lived in Pipewellgate. Some sublet part of a single room, and between 20 and 40 families shared one 'privy' or 'ashpit'. When cholera broke out, carters took away up to 700 loads of excrement from poorer streets, 'without exhausting' the 'offensive matter'.

Thomas Oliver, Plan of Newcastle and Gateshead, 1851.

Seventy-eight families lived in 14 houses in Leonard's Court, off upper High Street, and one in 20 died there. Elsewhere, 120 died in one block of buildings, three out of 30 died in one house and three others died in a cellar. In one street, 15 of the 488 inhabitants died, ten of them in cellars excavated from an 'accumulation of refuse'. Overall, 387 of the 433 who died in the Borough were in the town, including 29 comparatively well off ratepayers, some of whom lived in 'notoriously unhealthy districts'; yet there were no deaths in the 'best parts'. In Newcastle, 1,527 out of 80,000 inhabitants died. In Tynemouth, the Local Board of Health had been active, and 12 people died out of 30,000 .[26]

The Great Fire, 14 October 1854.

In 1854, Hillgate and part of Pipewellgate in Gateshead, and several streets at the west end of Newcastle quayside, burned down. Thousands of poor people living near the Tyne were made homeless.[27]

George Hawks and George Crawshay's ironworks, foundries and engineering factory at New Greenwich, east of Gateshead, employed over two thousand workers.[28] Small *colliers* – sea-going vessels – could anchor near its staithes, but *keels* – barges manned by *keelmen* – carried coal to the larger colliers nearer the river mouth.

Hawks, Crawshay & Sons Iron Works.

Workers' lives were still cheap. In 1854, a cart carrying a large piece of iron and an iron pan crushed a man to death at Hawks', but an inquest jury blamed the victim and returned a verdict of 'accidental death'. In 1855, Hawks' invested in Shipcote Colliery at Sunderland Road end, off High Street, and carters took coal to local houses. Mining stopped in 1856 and 1857, but resumed in spring 1858,[29] and by now the colliery probably had a waggonway down to the Tyne.

George Ridley had been 'tiring of underground work' for years, and may have done other work since 1853, the year his sister Mary was born. Probably in 1858, George got a job at Shipcote Colliery as a *waggonman*,[30] in charge of a set of wagons going up and down the railway line to the riverside staithes.[31] He was single, and still lived with his parents, who now had several children bringing in wages.

William IV had reigned between 1830 and 1837, and at some point a large building at 254 High Street, half a mile up from the Tyne, became the William IV Inn. In the 1840s, houses were erected around a stone quarry on Mr Grahamsley's land, behind the Inn,[32] but Grahamsley Street was unlit up to 1850.[33] In 1851, most residents were artisans and better-off workers, but eight people in two saddlers' households lived at No. 1, which was on the south side. In 1853, three people in the street died of cholera, and one was near No. 1.[34] In 1854, during the Crimean War, David Pringle at No. 2 wrote an anti-Russian poem, which appeared in a Newcastle paper.[35] The street was complete by 1858, [36] and a photograph taken 40 years or so later shows the three-storey houses on the north side.

In spring 1858, houses in Grahamsley Street cost over £180 to buy, and ten shillings a week to rent. That summer, 'Dr Airey', the 'Great American Lecturer' and 'Wonder of the Medical world', advertised in the *Newcastle Courant* that

Gateshead Libraries

William IV Inn and part of north Grahamsley Street.

'Mr George Ridley, 1, Grahamsley-street, Gateshead' had been 'Cured of a bad cough and difficulty breathing for twelve months, by DR AIREY in one week'. However, in 1859, 'Dr Airey' had to pay a £20 in Bristol for practising without medical qualifications.[37]

In summer 1860, James Robinson, Shipcote Colliery's old horsekeeper, was walking along the waggonway incline, when six wagons broke away, apparently because of a faulty rope socket. He suffered a crushed thigh and severe injuries to his head and neck, and though someone took him to Newcastle Infirmary, he soon died. At the inquest, the jury's verdict was 'accidental death'. The waggoner was not named in the newspaper report;[38] but after 'about three years' at Shipcote Colliery, George Ridley had a similar 'accident'.

> While riding, as usual, his train of wagons down the incline, (upon which his duties principally lay), by some breakage or

mishap, the wagons became unmanageable, and, being no longer under control, rushed at great speed down the incline. To save himself as much as possible from the danger threatening him, George jumped from his stand on the runaway wagons, but, in doing so, unfortunately got himself severely crushed and injured.

He 'lay, incapable of work', for 'a long time', and 'when at last he began to recover, his strength was so shattered' that he was 'totally unfitted' for 'anything like regular work'.[39] He had previously won a hat at a 'benefit' night at the Wheat Sheaf Inn in Newcastle, for being 'the best amateur comic singer'. His 'abilities' were 'of a superior order, but were 'only indulged in for a pastime'.[40] Now he was 'forced to seek a new means of earning a livelihood', he 'fell back' on his 'powers' of performance, 'especially of Irish comic and old Tyneside songs (in which he excelled)'.[41]

2 Balmbra's

John Balmbra was born in Alnwick, Northumberland, around 1808. By 1836, he was a 'licensed victualler' in Newcastle,[42] and he was landlord of the Wheat Sheaf Inn, 3 & 4 Cloth Market, by 1840.[43] The place became a 'sporting crib', where people organised foot races, horse races and boxing;[44] and by 1845 it had a 'Music Saloon'.[45] In summer 1846, Balmbra had a beer tent on the Town Moor during the races,[46] and in autumn he advertised that 'increasing Patronage' had necessitated 'extensive Alterations and Improvements', in 'a Style scarcely to be surpassed by the first-rate London houses'. 'Every social and rational amusement' would be provided, and the 'CONCERT ROOM' would 'open for the Season' at 8 o'Clock' on 2 November. He had 'engaged such a Galaxy of talent as will realize the Expectation of his most sanguine Friends', [47] and they included a local musician.

In the 1790s, Joseph Sessford had run a school in the Castle Garth, but he used the birch and cane too often and lost pupils like the future showman, Billy Purvis.[48] From 1801, Sessford was a clock- and watch-maker in the Groat Market, and in 1813, his wife, Eleanor, bore a son who they called John. By 1841, 28-year-old 'Jack' was landlord of the Angel Inn, Butcher Bank, and played piano to entertain the drinkers.[49] In 1844, he played at a 'Musical Melange' in the Music Hall, Nelson Street, to raise money for the striking pitmen.[50] By 1845, he had the Lord Nelson in Trafalgar Street, but he had left by 1847,[51] and played piano at 'Balmbra's'.[52]

John Balmbra invested more capital and the *Newcastle*

Guardian reported that 'when the Decorations and Improvements in progress are in a state of completion' his 'Music Saloon' would 'vie with any out of the Metropolis for splendour and elegance'. Entrance cost fourpence, but that included 'refreshment'. The 'Vocal Department' was 'highly respectable', and the 'Instrumental Department' was 'far above mediocrity, as such names as Sessford as a Pianist, and Charles Easthope as a Violinist, will at once verify'. Sessford's 'vocal accompaniments take equally upon his delighted auditory' and 'Mr Easthope's solo playing upon the Violin must be heard to be appreciated'.[53] They were not the only local talent.

James Spiers spent six months in jail for larceny in Northumberland in 1843 and married at Alnwick in 1845. He had been a member of Billy Purvis's company, and specialised in Irish songs;[54] but in 1847, aged around 27, he was at Balmbra's. According to the *Newcastle Guardian*, James H. Spiers was 'a finished comic singer', but he was no longer singing for 'a mixed and heterogeneous multitude', and 'requires a little of the polish, and a little less of the grimace'. In addition, Balmbra should reconsider his policy of 'excluding the admission of the fairer portion of society' – women.[55]

Thomas Boutland was born around 1808. He became a 'Cabinet Maker', and by 1841, aged 33, he lived in New Court, Westgate Street, Newcastle, with his wife, young son and a male servant. In 1847, the London entertainment paper, *The Era*, noted of Balmbra's.

> The singing is far superior to what we are accustomed to hear in most provincial towns, especially the execution of the music allotted to Madame C.C. Gill and Mr. John Sessford. Mr. Thomas Boutland is a good musician, and the comic humour of Mr. S. Bennette creates much laugher. We understand the respected host

has expended £700 in the building of this splendid saloon, and we trust the public will patronise him in his speculation.

In 1848, 'J. Spiers and J. Ward, the two comic singers' were at the Wheat Sheaf, and it was 'well attended';[56] but later that year there was a problem.

Simon Herman, an attorney's clerk, was 'in the habit of attending Mr Balmbra's concert', and summonsed him for assault. Herman acknowledged that he was 'hissing' one singer, but then he was 'seized by the defendant, struck', 'thrown upon the ground' and 'turned to the door'. Balmbra testified that he had 'remonstrated with the complainant for his ungentlemanly behaviour' and 'threatened him with expulsion if he did not behave himself better'.

> On the night in question, during the singing of a national song, the complainant, who was a foreigner, took occasion to display his rudeness, and an uproar in the house was the result. On complainant's refusal to withdraw, he was compelled to take him by the collar, and drag him out. He did not, however, strike him.

Balmbra paid a fine of two shillings and sixpence, and five shillings costs; but the magistrates refused Herman's solicitor's request to order him to take the summons down from his Concert Room wall.[57]

In spring 1849, *The Era* noted the international artistes in the company at Balmbra's and its growing reputation.

> This splendid and popular place of entertainment continues to enjoy the patronage of the good folks of Newcastle, the great attraction at present being the unique and astonishing performances of that clever equilibrist and gymnasia, Signor Carlo Alberto. A Mr Mellor, an American, represents the Yankee and Nigger characters to the very life, and stands pre-eminently and deservedly popular with the admirers of such

faithful delineations. Miss Collis is the leading cantatrice, Miss Mason, as the elegant and graceful representative of Terpsichore, Mr J Spiers, the inimitable delineator of the broad grin; Mr Ses[s]ford, the accomplished baritone and local vocalist and pianist; and Mr C. Easthope, as leader of the orchestra and prototype of the celebrated Paganini, all stand deservedly popular. But indeed all the performers both vocal and instrumental of this select company, nightly merit the applause with which they are honoured, and bid fair to bring this elegant place of resort into that repute which few rival provincial establishments can presume to lay claim to, and from which we hear, the spirited proprietor, Mr Balmbra, is reaping so golden a harvest.[58]

Late that year, Balmbra donated an evening's takings to the widows and orphans of drowned lifeboat crewmen.[59]

Early in 1850, *The Era* noted that the Wheat Sheaf was 'well-conducted' and 'continues to receive that patronage which it deserves'.

This popular establishment continues to increase in attraction, the succession of novelties which the enterprising and indefatigable manager brings forward for the entertainment of his patrons drawing every night crowded and respectable audiences. The utmost harmony and good feeling pervades the company, each member seeming to vie with each other, not only in promoting his or her professional reputation and respectability, but the interest of an establishment which has for years sustained a celebrity surpassed by few, if any, in the provinces.[60]

In summer, the *Newcastle Journal* reported on Newcastle races.

There was, as usual, a great number of tents erected in the usual locality, stretching eastward along the Moor from nearly

> opposite the winning chair; and many were remarkable for the taste displayed in their decorations, especially at the principle entrance. Mr. Balmbra, of the Wheat Sheaf, deserves great credit for having led the way in the march of improvement in this respect.

The entrance to his tent was a 'beautiful portico, surmounted by a "golden sheaf"'.[61] In autumn, the 'very attractive' 'bill of fare' at Balmbra's drew 'crowded houses' and 'business continued good'. 'Mr. J. Sessford' was one of the 'principle performers' and the company had a 'very steady run' up to Christmas.[62]

A Bewick workshop illustration of Newcastle Races.

By 1851, John Sessford, 'Professor of Music', aged 38, lived in Percy Court, off Percy Street, with 28-year-old Mary from Gateshead. She was evidently his second wife, since John junior, a gilder, was 18, and Mary, aged 16, was a 'servant'. Three children, aged between six and ten, were at school, and two others were four and two. Charles Easthope, a 32-year-old 'Professor of Music' from Wolverhampton, lived next door with his Newcastle-born wife, Margaret, and two children. John Balmbra, aged 37, and 35-year-old Isabella, his Newcastle-born wife, lived at the Wheat Sheaf.

Eighteen-year-old Mary Windley from Woolwich in Kent was a 'House Maid' and 23-year-old Ann Braban from Byker Hill was the cook. Thirty-year-old Mary Ann Gibbon, a 'Visitor' from London, was a 'Vocalist'. Songs travelled further.

Stephen Foster's *Old Folks at Home* crossed the Atlantic rapidly. A boy who went to Balmbra's was delighted with 'the singing of "Way down upon the Swanny River, " then newly written', and 'not unfrequently revisited the hall', where Sessford, the 'chairman',

> sang many a charming song, and amongst others a farewell to emigrants, 'God speed ye all ye hopeful band', and a somewhat sad invitation to 'Come, come with me to the Old Kirkyard.' I have heard some excellent singing there – 'Hail Smiling Morn, ' and others.[63]

In spring, Balmbra had a 'very strong' company, and late that year his Concert Room was 'undergoing very extensive alterations', to be able to accommodate 'upwards of 2,000 persons'.[64] Sessford sang in a Grand Concert of English Secular Music at Christmas, but evidently needed the 'kind permission of Mr Balmbra' to do so.[65]

By 1852, 19,000 Newcastle people – over a fifth of the population – survived on poor relief; but there were 501 places to buy alcohol.[66] In spring, *The Era* noted that Balmbra's Royal Music Saloon 'fills to overflow each evening'. In summer, in *The Era*, he requested 'the patronage of his numerous friends and the public in general' at his 'large and elegantly fitted up TENT' on the Moor, which was 'well stocked with all the necessary comforts required for the inward man'. (He did not mention the 'inward woman.') In the evening, the Royal Promenade Concert Room offered the 'NE PLUS ULTRA of MORAL, INSTRUCTIVE and RATIONAL AMUSEMENT, consisting of SONGS, DUETS, GLEES, CHORUSES, and TERPSICHORIAN EXERCISES,

BALLETS D'ACTION, &c., by the most talented Company of Artistes ever concentrated in one establishment'.

> The ROOM and SCENERY have been greatly enlarged by that talented Artist, Mr. JOHN OGILVIE, from Aberdeen, and assistants; and for beauty of decorations and comfort is not equalled by any other public place of amusement. In fact neither time nor expense has been spared to make this place worthy the large patronage of a liberal and discerning public.

'First-class Professionals' were 'required', and 'no others will be treated with'.

Late in 1853, *The Era* reported that 'Balmbra's Promenade Concert Hall' was 'nightly well attended'. The 'proprietor of this unique establishment' had been 'well repaid for the great amount of capital he has laid out in the enlargement, decoration, &c., by the crowded audiences who nightly assemble, and testify by their heart plaudits the talents' of 11 performers. The 'Promenade Music Saloon' was 'well patronised by a very respectable audience'.[67]

In spring 1855, Patrick Conolly tried to pass counterfeit sixpences at the Wheat Sheaf; but Isabella Balmbra took him to court and he got six months' hard labour.[68] In summer, James Spiers' benefit night was a 'bumper'. In spring 1856, John Balmbra advertised in *The Era*.

> WANTED. – A LEADING VIOLINIST, who can read at sight and thoroughly understands Concert room business. None but steady men need apply, and testimonials required.
>
> Applications, stating lowest terms, with stamped and directed envelope, will meet with prompt attention.

Early in 1857, Balmbra's was 'well attended'. One artiste advertised in *The Era*, asking for 'letters respecting Engagements' to be sent there, 'post paid'.[69] In spring, Charles Easthope died in Bayley Street.[70] Late that year,

Balmbra described himself as one who 'seeks by Music and Poetry to promote virtue and truth, and aid in the progress of human improvement'.[71] Soon after, he became President of Newcastle Licensed Victuallers' Association.[72] Thomas Boutland had a 'Farewell' benefit concert at Balmbra's;[73] and when he died in Portland Place in 1859, an obituary described him as a 'cabinet-maker'.[74] John Sessford, 'Professor of Music', and his large family lived at 10 Percy Court.[75]

Fifteen-year-old Archibald Reed visited the Wheat Sheaf. The concert room on the first floor 'extended nearly to Grey Street' and the stage at the Grey Street end was 'facing west'. In front were 'the best seats – boxes so called – and the remainder at a convenient price to suit the working classes'. Balmbra 'conducted this place of amusement in a most creditable style', [76] but he faced competition.

James Donald was born in Scotland around 1801. In 1826 his 25-year-old wife, Janet, bore a son they called Adam Elphinstone. By 1830, a second son called John was born in Newcastle. By 1834, James had a watchmaker's workshop at 103 Side, and he was a watchmaker and jeweller at 34 Mosley Street by 1838. He was still there in 1844; but he made chronometers and watches at 80 Grey Street and lived at 7 Marlborough Crescent in 1847. By 1850, the family had moved to 8 Albion Place.[77] Adam was the Provincial Grand Secretary of the Provincial Grand Lodge of Northumberland and Berwick-on-Tweed Freemasons and had a watchmaker and jeweller's shop in Grey Street. In 1851, he married 24-year-old Margaret Forster Jamieson.[78] They lived with his parents, but James evidently retired by 1852, and John ran 80 Grey Street. By 1855, Adam had shops at 54 Grey Street and Gibson Street.[79] By 1856, he owned the Grainger Hotel, [80] at 36 Grainger Street, on the corner of Market Street;[81] but he had given up watch making by 1857, and focussed on what had become the Grainger Hotel and Billiard Rooms by 1859.[82]

By 1860, leading artistes went from the Arcade Music Hall in Sunderland to the Wheat Sheaf in Newcastle. Late that year, Balmbra advertised in *The Era* for 'every description of Concert Room talent, of the first class': 'Enclose stamp for a reply'.[83] Donald announced that it would cost sixpence to enter the Grainger Hotel's licensed 'Concert Supper and Billiard Room' on Christmas Eve,[84] and early in 1861, Balmbra advertised impressively in the Newcastle directory.

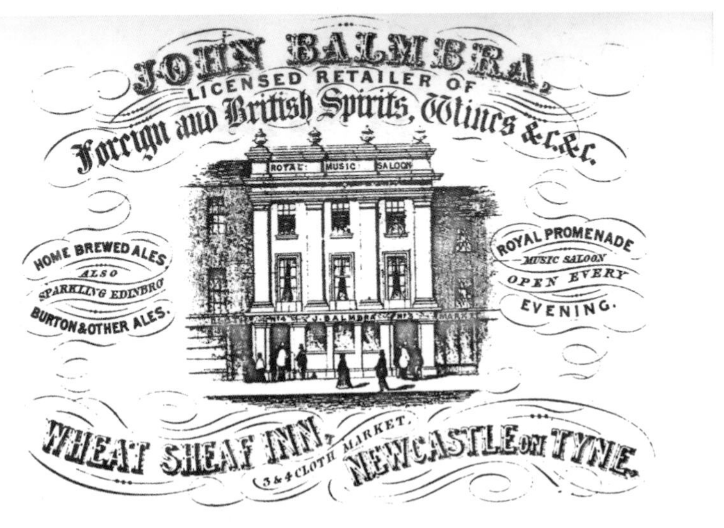

Capital investment was becoming crucial to music saloons and the support of working-class voters was crucial to ambitious politicians.

3 The Gateshead vocalist

John Cowen was born in 1774. He became a blacksmith at Crowley's ironworks in Winlaton, five miles west of Newcastle, a firm that made chains for slaves. In 1799, he married Mary Newbiggin from Ryton. Their son, Joseph, was born at Greenside in 1800, and when John later began working for himself as a chain maker, Joseph became his apprentice.[85] In 1819, the massacre of peaceful political reformers in Manchester became known, sardonically, as 'Peterloo'. Mary led a branch of Female Reformers to the Newcastle Town Moor protest demonstration and Joseph led the Winlaton Northern Political Union's 'class' of blacksmiths. That year, Mary Cowen junior married Anthony Forster, a brick manufacturer at Blaydon.[86] In 1822, Joseph Cowen married Mary Newton, the daughter of 'a neighbour in his own social position', but he managed his brother-in-law's brick works by 1825. He enlarged the business,[87] and patented a very successful firebrick, which brought him enough capital to buy land, a colliery, a small railway and loading staithes on the Tyne.

Joseph Cowen junior was born in a large house near Blaydon Burn brickworks in 1829. In 1832, Joseph senior was a member of the Northern Political Union, which played an important role in securing the Reform Act; and in 1839 Winlaton was the local 'headquarters' of radical Chartists. Joseph junior went to a boarding school in Burnopfield. Later, he became a pupil of Henry Anderson, the former schoolmaster at Crowley's ironworks, and then he attended Mr Week's Academy at Ryton. In 1845, aged 16, he entered the University of Edinburgh. He corresponded with Giuseppe

Mazzini, the Italian revolutionary nationalist, and left the university, without completing his degree, in 1847. He returned to Winlaton and founded a Literary, Scientific and Mechanics' Institute, which was 'open to all, irrespective of their mark or station' and 'without regard to their political or religious sentiments'. Only men could serve on the committee, but half had to be workers. In 1848, the year of revolutions in Europe, Thomas Vallance, a keelman, became President of the new Blaydon and Stella Mechanical Institute, and Joseph Cowen junior was its Secretary. In 1850, he financed the *Red Republican*, which published the first translation of Marx and Engels' *Communist Manifesto*. By 1852, Blaydon and Stella Mechanics' Institute had a purpose-built hall, with educational and recreational facilities. In 1854, Cowen junior hosted the Italian revolutionary nationalist, Giuseppe Garibaldi, who spoke at Winlaton Mechanics' Institute. Cowen also financed the radical *Northern Tribune* and founded the Northern Republican Brotherhood.[88] He married Jane Thompson, the daughter of

Stella Hall c.1900, where Joseph Cowen lived from 1855.

a County Durham coal owner, and by 1855 they lived in Stella Hall, an Elizabethan mansion near Blaydon.[89]

Joseph Cowen.

Cowen junior hired musicians for concerts at Blaydon Mechanics' Institute and loaned the family piano. He hosted the revolutionary republicans Felice Orsini and Lajos Kossuth at Stella Hall, and both became honorary life members of the Institute.[90] In 1857, Cowen began buying shares in the *Newcastle Chronicle*.[91] In January 1858, he founded the Northern Reform Union. Days later, Orsini failed to assassinate the French Emperor, Louis Napoleon.[92] Cowen probably financed the attempt and he spoke about it to 'rapturous applause' at Blaydon Institute.[93] Ninety per cent of Blaydon's inhabitants were members. By 1859, he controlled the *Newcastle Chronicle* and staffed it with radicals and republicans.[94] He hosted the revolutionary republican Mazzini and became Secretary of the Northern Union of Mechanics' Institutes. In 1860, the *Chronicle* advertised for volunteers to fight alongside General Garibaldi for an Italian republic.[95]

John and Isabella Balmbra still lived at the Wheat Sheaf, with two servants. Twenty-three-year-old Elizabeth Eltringham was from Durham and 18-year-old Margaret Collins was from Carlisle.

By 1861, Newcastle's population was 109,000 . The town stretched away to the north, east and west, and its economic, political and cultural institutions dominated all of Tyneside and its hinterland.

John Storey's view of Newcastle upon Tyne in the Reign of Queen Victoria, 1862.

Gateshead's 33,000 inhabitants lived in 4,259 houses, at an average of almost eight per dwelling.

George Ridley's uncle, the 'Labourer', Thomas Stephenson, and his 33-year-old wife, Martha, lived at 98 Charles Street, Gateshead, with three children aged two, seven and eleven. George's older brother, John, a 'Coal Miner', lived in Pipewellgate, Gateshead, with Elena, his 25-year-old wife, Hannah, aged three, and Elizabeth, aged six months. George's older sister, Elizabeth, had left Tyneside or died.

At 1 Grahamsley Street, Gateshead, Matthew senior, a 'Rope-Maker', and Frances, had taken in her 69-year-old mother, Elizabeth Stephenson. Six-year-old Benjamin was a 'Scholar', as were eight-year-old Mary and 12-year-old

Crowded and dilapidated conditions in Pipewellgate, Gateshead, from the Tyne, 1879.

David. Fifteen-year-old 'Stephen[son]' was a 'Coney [rabbit-skin] Cutter', 21-year-old Young was a 'wire rope maker', 24-year-old Matthew was a 'Coney Cutter' at a 'Hat Manufactory' and 26-year-old George was a 'Vocalist'.

Early in June, *The Era* reported that Balmbra had engaged 'Mr. G. Ridley' for the Wheat Sheaf as an 'Irish Comic Vocalist'.[96]

Soon after, the Cowen family revived horse races on Blaydon Island, a quarter of a mile from the railway station. The four-mile journey from Newcastle took 15 minutes.[97] At 1.30pm on race day, Newcastle & Carlisle Railway Company guards in Newcastle Central Station, wearing scarlet frock coats and silk chimney-pot hats, crammed ten passengers into second-class carriages designed for eight and hooked up mineral wagons and vans to carry more. A second train left at 2.00pm. The *Chronicle* reporter did not like being 'up to the neck in balloons of crinoline' or having to put his pipe out. He believed that it was better to travel directly to the course on the roof of a horse-drawn omnibus, with a 'smoking weed', even though it took 45 minutes, cost sixpence, and the companies 'might harness better cattle if they wished to assure passengers of the safety of their means of transport'. That evening, the Anniversary Soirée at Whickham Mechanics' Institute was 'agreeably varied by the introduction of a number of songs – comic and sentimental, the former contributed by Mr. Ridley', whose 'characteristic drolleries' caused 'the greatest merriment'.

The *Chronicle* reported that 'Mr. Ridley' was engaged to perform at Adam E. Donald's Grainger Concert and Supper Rooms in Newcastle. The 'admirable singer of local songs' performed at the Blaydon Mechanics' Institute's Annual Soirée and 'delighted the company' with 'comic delineations'. Late in June, an omnibus left the Wheat Sheaf in Newcastle for Swalwell and Derwenthaugh Mechanics' Institute's Annual Soirée, where seats cost a shilling. The 'comic and local songs by Mr. Ridley' were 'well received' and he was 'an especial favourite with the juvenile portion of the audience'.

In July, the *Chronicle* report on Newcastle Town Moor races noted that the 'representative of literature, whose wares consisted of ballads fixed on the side of one of the tents', had 'rendered "Larry O'Gaff" and "Highland Mary" to anybody who choosed to buy' old-fashioned Irish and Scots lyrics.[98] Underhand had won the Northumberland Plate three times, and the Gateshead fiddler Jimmy Hill had composed a tune in his honour,[99] so Underhand was 100 to 30 favourite. Joey Jones was 10 to 1,[100] and his win 'was a great surprise to the Public generally, but a more popular victory could not have been achieved' and his owners 'landed a great stake'.[101] *The*

Era reported that 'Mr Ridley, late of Balmbra's Concert Hall', had an engagement at the Grainger Concert and Supper Rooms.[102] There, he 'brought out his first Local song', [103] set to an Irish rebel tune.

JOEY JONES.
"PAT OF MULLINGAR.'

Aw'm gan te sing te ye a sang, if ye'll but list te me,
Aw divent intend te keep ye lang, an' that ye plainly see;
It's all aboot young Joey Jones, he wun the Northumberland plate,
He was bred at Deckham Hall, just up throo the gate.

CHORUS:—
For he jogs along, he canter'd along, he lick'd them all se fine
He was bred at Geytshead, he's the pride o' coaly Tyne.

Joey ran at the spring meeting, he was beaten by the Jim,
Hadlow, that belangs Gaylad, said Joey wasn't game;
So they sent him off te Richmond, 'twas knawn he wasn't right,
Then Watson fetch'd him here an' gov them a regular Yorkshire bite.

Noo when the horses started an' was cumin past the stand,
Sum shooted oot for Peggy Taft, sum for Underhand;
An' when they reach'd the top o' the hill, Doyle heard Tom Aldcroft say
"Aw dare lay a fiver that aw win the plate to day!'

Cumin roond the Morpeth turn, Joey keepin up his fame,
Says Doyle te Tommy Aldcroft 'noo what's yor little game?
Says Aldcroft 'aw mean te win the plate this vary day!
'Yes, but, says Doyle, 'it's Joey Jones, a fiver aw will lay."

Number eleven was puttin up, the people stood amazed,
Fobert he luik'd vary white, an' Jackson almost crazed;
Little Osborne luik'd for his Wildman, an' Sharpe for Volatile
Doefoot got a nasty kick, an' Joey wun in style.

George Ridley's Local Song Book.

'As a public singer', Ridley was 'highly gifted', with a 'fine voice' and 'great powers of mimicry', and he 'swayed his audience at his will'. His singing talents, the first-hand insider's report and the 'local popularity of the subject', made his song 'a great success'.[104]

A decade earlier, Ned Corvan was Tyneside's first full-time professional singer and 'local' songwriter. In *Snooks the Artist*, set to *Billy Nutts*, he satirised Gateshead Corporation's illiterate Bellman, John Higgins, or 'J[ohnn]y L[ui]k up', as a man who would find a lost child, but only for a shilling.[105] Higgins earned £10 a year, but had 'a good business as a house agent' on the side; and on his retirement in 1860, instead of a pension, he got 'a medal in recognition of his consistent teetotalism during a long course of years'. Some thought him 'a really worthy man, ' but acknowledged that 'in sundry respects' he was 'an original'.[106] He died in early summer 1861.

For his second 'local' song, Ridley used a US blackface minstrel tune, which E.W. Mackney had composed in 1859 for *Sally Come Up*. T. Ramsay's lyrics noted that her 'Massa' had 'gone to town' and stressed what he considered to be her least attractive features, but it was a hit for G. Swaine Buckley.[107] Ridley dressed 'in character' as a Gateshead bellman, [108] came on stage, accompanied by a disconsolate child in rags, [109] and imitated Higgins's 'peculiarities'.[110]

JOHNNY LUIK-UP! AIR.—SALLY COME UP.

Thor was a bit laddy lost the tuther day,
And doon the kee he stray'd away,
The muther was cryin' hard they say,
So she fund oot Johnny the bellman,
Says she 'gan roond the toon,
Aw'll gie ye half-a-croon,
For if he's not fund it'll be maw ruin,
Wor Jimmy he'll surely kill me.

Chorus.—Johnny luik up, Johnny luik doon,
Johnny gans wandrin roond the toon,
He'll find yor kid for half-a-croon, will Johnny Luik-up the bellman.

Johnny's a chep that'll not take a job,
Unless he's sure that he'll get a bob,
An' when he shoots he twists his gob,
Thor's neyn can shoot like Johnny.

Noo the lads they de him scoff,
He hes such a nasty cough,
Aw doot sum fine day he'll pop off,
Then we'll loss poor Johnny.

Before he started te ring the bell,
He used te gan wi' young lambs te sell,
He was a candy man as aw hear tell,
Noo a perfect cure is Johnny.
An' he used te sell claes pins,
An' sumtimes bairns' rings
An' a lottery bag he used te hev',
Mair blanks then owt had Johnny.

In these days he a was a regular brick,
When he seld the munkeys up the stick,
An' candy for the bairns te lick,
A tin trumpet then had Johnny.
Ye shud only seen him blaw,
He fairly bangs them a',
It's like a cochin-china's craw,
An' sic a beak hes Johnny.

Sum thowt Johnny was rang in his mind,
When he used te gan wi' yor scissors te grind
For hard wark he was niver inclined,
For it niver agreed wi' Johnny.
Aw 've seen him on a winter's day,
When he's been shullin snaw away
Fra' shopkeepers' doors he'd lick a score,
The soup kitchen prop is Johnny.

Noo aw propose when Johnny dies,
That they take oot one of his eyes,
An' put it inte cock-eyed Tom that sells the pies,
Then we'll niver loss sight of Johnny.
So lads just gie yor lasses a treat,
Te this place sum uther neet,
Aw'll gie ye the Bobby on his beat,
An' the life of Johnny the bellman.

George Ridley's Local Song Book.

A *candyman* usually cried 'here you have –real genyouwine candy – mixt up wi' sugar an' brandy, with the real oil of mint'. He carried an old tea-board on his head, covered with penny 'toy-lambs', who had cotton wool stuck on their backs and long curled horns made from tin chippings.[111] Ridley and his audiences knew that *candyman* was a term of abuse in pit villages,[112] and that Higgins was a bosses' lackey, fraudster and scrounger, who exploited distressed mothers by demanding over half a labourer's weekly pay to find a child; so the song was a 'palpable hit' with 'crowded audiences gathering to hear him',[113] and his 'success was unbounded'.[114]

Ridley called Higgins a 'perfect cure', after *The Perfect Cure*, a satirical piece sung by James Henry Stead, a veteran of Billy Purvis's show, at Weston's Music Hall in London. Ridley's invitation to 'lads' to bring 'yor lasses' suggests that music saloon and concert hall audiences were mainly single young men who liked to hear a public officer being ridiculed, and the penultimate line of *Johnny Luik-Up* linked to his third song, which confirms this anti-authority appeal. Ridley set it to *The Cure* and dressed as a police sergeant.

THE BOBBY CURE. AIR.—"THE CURE."

Oh lads aw've turned a bobby noo,
And disn't maw dress luik neat,
Aw've a greet moosetash abuve me gob,
And aw'm on the Gateshead beat;
Noo all the jobs thor is aw've tried,
But neyn aw can endure,
So noo aw've join'd the Gateshead force,
And the kids calls me the cure.

Aw mind the first neet that aw was on,
It was doon in Pipergate,
An Irish row had started there,
Thinks aw aw'll knaw me fate,
Aw rushes doon and collars one,
We fell in a common sewer,
As aw crawl'd oot the kids did shoot
"Just twig poor Bobby the cure."

The next neet aw was on the bottle bank
Aw was on for a reglar spree.
There aw fell in win a nice young lass,
She went inte the GOAT wi' me,

Noo each of us hes a glass o' rum,
At her expence yor sure,
She was a married wife an' her man pop'd in
And he mug'd poor Bobby the cure.

Aw hook'd it off win a sheepish luik,
And her man reported me,
The inspector com' and says " noo Bobby
This wark it winna de!"
Aw was taken before the committee,
And was heavy fined aw's sure,
And still when aw's on the Oakwellgate beat
The kids calls me a cure.

The next neet aw was on the Windmill Hills
Forget it aw niver shall,
They war' smashin' the windows there like fun
And pushin doon the walls,
Aw tuik ten te the stashon hoose,
Withoot ony help aw'm sure,
Aw got these two stripes on maw coat,
And they still call me a cure.

A bobby's the canniest job in the world,
He gets all his drink for nowt;
Aw'm what they call drill sarjant noo,
Maw claes aw ready bowt;
So noo aw've teld ye all maw tricks,
Ye'll pity me aw'm sure,
And niver call me when aw's on maw beat,
And say there gans the cure.

George Ridley's Local Song Book.

Children sang *The Bobby Cure* and *Johnny Luik-Up!* 'as they ran about the streets'. Ridley had 'engagements at the various concert halls in the north', and 'everywhere he was a favourite';[115] but he faced serious competition for engagements at the larger halls.

4 The Tyne Concert Hall

Samuel Stanley had travelled all over Europe as a general's servant, and was present at the battle of Waterloo in 1815. George William Stanley was born in London in 1823. As a boy, he played in an amateur minor company, and by 1843 he managed a provincial theatre. He went on to act in Midland theatres and then in leading theatres across Britain.[116] Around 1850, in Dublin, Emilie Bache, the daughter of Scarborough merchant captain, was a member of the same company. She was ten years his junior, but they married. Later, they performed in Cork, Belfast, Edinburgh, Glasgow, Bradford, Manchester, Hull and elsewhere. Stanley managed theatres in Cork, Bury, Stockport, Berwick, Jedburgh and South Shields, but in 1854, he was a leading actor at Newcastle Theatre Royal,[117] and remained there until 1856.[118] In 1857, Sangar Brothers leased the huge wooden circus in Neville Street, near Central Station, and other showmen later followed suit. In summer 1860, Stanley leased it and applied for a dramatic licence, but the Theatre Royal proprietors objected and the magistrates refused,[119] twice. So he borrowed money,[120] got a licence from the Gateshead magistrates for a 'temporary theatre' in East Street,[121] and then a licence from South Shields magistrates for the Central Hall, Chapter Row, over Christmas.

In June 1861, at Manors Police Court in Newcastle, Stanley applied for a six-month licence to stage 'operatic and amphitheatre' performances at the circus, which was owned by a contractor called Robson. In eighty years, the town's population had grown five-fold, and there was still only one theatre, but the magistrates refused.[122] In July, Stanley announced in Cowen's *Newcastle Daily Chronicle* that the 'commodious building' in Neville Street was 'undergoing extensive Alterations' to 'render it equal to any, and superior to most Establishments of its kind in the Provinces'. The internal Scenic Embellishments and Decorations were 'from the pencil of a distinguished Artist', the 'Vocal and Instrumental performers' would be the 'Most Popular and Talented Ladies and Gentlemen in the Musical Profession', and 'neither expense nor trouble will be spared to make the entire Establishment in every way worthy of the patronage of the people of Tyneside'. Seats would cost threepence in the gallery, sixpence in the 'Area and Side elevations for two thousand Persons' and a shilling in the 'handsome Box Promenade'. Stanley invited tenders for the franchise to serve alcohol in the 'extensive Refreshment saloon' adjoining the main building.[123]

The Tyne Concert Hall opened on 24 August. The *Chronicle* reported that it was 'besieged with an eager crowd' and 'numbers were turned away from the pit and gallery doors'. The interior had changed.

> On the north side, where the boxes formerly were, an extremely neat and commodious stage has been erected, with a large orchestra in front. The centre, which constitutes the pit, has been fitted with comfortable looking seats, with backs attached, while the whole of the raised seats on each side have been thrown together and form the gallery. The promenade is open all round the building, with seats on each side, and is the best part of the house, 'the boxes'.

Alcohol was available in the adjoining 'large and comfortable refreshment rooms'.

The 'first-Class Company' from 'the principal Metropolitan and Provincial Music Halls' included 'Artists in

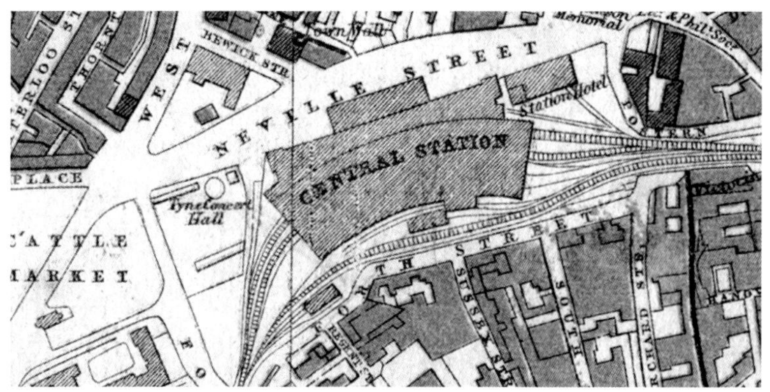

Top, Christie's New Plan of Newcastle and Gateshead, 1865.

Below, detail from John Storey's 'Newcastle upon Tyne in the Reign of Queen Victoria', 1862. The concert hall is the round building.

every Department, Vocal and instrumental'. The Tyne held 2, 840, and was the largest hall in the region, but had 'crowded houses nightly'.[124] The conservative *Newcastle Guardian* noted snootily that 'skilled musicians' had failed to 'establish cheap concerts', since they were 'above the comprehension of the working men'; yet 'Concert Halls, or Casinos', were 'springing up', and the Tyne, 'one of these singing places', attracted audiences of over 2,000 .[125]

In September, Stanley applied for a dramatic licence once again at Manors Police Court. His counsel pointed to the 'good behaviour shown by large numbers who frequented Mr Stanley's concert room'. Newcastle's Town Surveyor considered the building safe and the police had 'never had one complaint'. Counsel for the Theatre Royal proprietors and lessee opposed the application and the magistrates, including the Mayor and several aldermen, rejected it. Some people in the crowded courtroom showed a 'degree of disapprobation'.[126] Next day, the *Newcastle Guardian* reported that Hugh Smith's Victoria Rooms in Grey Street

Grey Street, the Theatre Royal in the distance, in 1860.

was a concert venue. It was 'the most comfortable looking and spacious in the town' and 'well patronised'. Stanley, accompanied by Joseph Cowen junior, [127] applied again for a one-year dramatic licence like the one that Manchester magistrates had granted to the Free Trade Hall. The Tyne could hold 'upwards of 3,000 persons' and Stanley wished to stage 'representations on the verge of the dramatic', without it becoming a 'regular Theatre'. The magistrates took five minutes to refuse his application, [128] so Stanley wrote to the *Newcastle Guardian*, noting that the bench appeared to have a 'stronger sympathy for the supposed interests of the proprietors of the Theatre Royal'.[129]

In October, George Ridley performed at 'The Popular Fortnightly Musical and Dramatic Entertainment' at Blaydon Mechanics' Institute. A 'Front Seat' cost a shilling, one in the 'Body of the Hall' was sixpence and entrance to the Gallery cost threepence. The *Chronicle* reported that 'Mr. Ridley' sang 'some of his excellent Local songs', including two 'of his own composing, to old favourite tunes, which were well received, and loudly encored' by a 'numerous audience'. Ridley's next engagement was at the Tyne. The *Chronicle* noted that his 'capabilities as a Local singer' were 'well known, and his popularity was 'quite equal to what we have had the pleasure of witnessing at other places', while the Tyne's audiences 'continue as numerous and orderly as they have always been'. On Saturday and Monday, it was 'crowded to the doors', which was 'rather beyond the usual', to see the 'popular Tyneside Vocalist', 'well-known local singer' and 'favourite member of Mr. Stanley's present company'.[130] John Balmbra needed artistes who could fill two thousand seats.

Tom Handford's career as an entertainer had begun around 1844.[131] In 1850, 'Mr Handford, the bango bone player and nigger dancer', was at the Derby Arms Casino in Nottingham. In 1854, The Brothers Handford, Tom and Joe, 'celebrated delineators of Negro life and manners', performed at the Midland Counties Music Hall in Birmingham and the East London Music Hall, where 'Mr. T.H.' was 'acknowledged to be the best Clog and Boot Dancer extant'. In 1856, The Brothers Handford were at Balmbra's Royal Music Saloon in Newcastle and 'every available place was filled to overflowing' on their benefit night. *The Era* saw this as 'certain proof of what good catering will do, when combined with such talent'. Balmbra's was 'nightly crowded' to hear their 'Nigger Melodies'.[132] Tom got married in Newcastle and in 1857 The Brothers Handford were 'the main attraction' at Balmbra's for two months. By 1858, Joe was a solo act, and Mr and Mrs Thomas Handford were a duo; but by 1861 Tom, the 'Black Diamond', also performed solo.[133]

That autumn, George Ridley wrote a song to support Stanley's campaign for a dramatic licence. He celebrated the Newcastle and Gateshead engineers who formed the core of the Tyne's audiences and named the engineering factory owners who established and led rifle corps;[134] but he lampooned the volunteer 'Noodles' for their incompetence and cowardice and their loyalty to officers who were reactionary coal owners.[135] The tune given for this song when it was later published does not fit the lyrics, and Vic Gammon believes that Ridley sang it to *Phoebe Morel, or I Had a Dream*, also known as *The Slaves' Dream*.

THE RIFLEMEN.

AIR.—"COAL BLACK ROSE."

Aw had a dream the uther neet when everything was still,
Aw thowt aw saw the rifles gan on the moor te drill;
Aw thowt aw saw Clinton's model band playin' the "Young
Recruit,"
And Sir John Fife given his men a walk oot.

CHORUS:—

Three cheers for STANLEY'S, lang may he shine!
For iv a' the concerts i' the toon thor's nyen can liek the TYNE.

Aw thowt aw saw Arimstrang's Engineers, wi' thor reed
jackets they luik neat,
They war' gan te meet the Gateshead corps alang Blackett
Street;
Then there was Allhueson's fra' the South Shore,
Wi' thor white belts aroond them, they're a vary smart corps.

Aw thowt aw saw the Noodles bould led on by Tommy Carr,
And the kids they wor cryin' "ye darnet gan te war!"
Thor was one fell off his horse and was cover'd ower wi' mud

He cried like ony bairn when his nose it started blood.

Aw thowt aw went te STANLEY's, just te spend an hour,
And aw saw Tom Handford dein the "Black Cure,"
He sung "Awd Bob Ridley," and danced wi' the clogs;
James cam' on wi' Joe and Tommy, then the Monkeys and
 the Dogs.

Aw thowt aw saw James Hodge, that's him that plays the
 base,
And the second fiddler te, noo he's in the reet place;
Bob Sanderson play'd sum' nice airs, wi' Aleck on the flute,
And Aleck says te Charley Coutts "will ye stand a gill of
 stout?"

Noo thor's Stephenson's lads and Hawthorn's they're vary
 often here,
May Hawks's lads and Abbot's lads niver want thor beer;
Thor's scores flocks' fra the railway shops, and Morrison's
 luikin' on;
The glass-hoose lads they blaw pipes lang, but Airmstrang's
 number one.

George Ridley's Local Song Book.

Tom Handford was willing to travel long distances for engagements, but Ridley stayed close to home and wrote about local heroes.

Harry Clasper was born in Dunston around 1820, but when he was a boy his parents moved the family to Jarrow and sent him to work in a pit. Later, he was a cinder-burner at Garsfield coke ovens, and around the age of 20 he became a wherryman. In his spare time, he built a lightweight 'sculler' boat, and in 1845, with two brothers and an uncle, he won the world championship on the Thames. In 1861, when Harry was in his early forties, he and his son John, Robert Chambers and Edward Winship won a race at the Thames Regatta.[136]

In his next song Ridley celebrated local rowers and John Oliver – 'Coffee Johnny' – who was 33 and almost two metres tall.[137] He had been a bare-knuckle fighter, capable of going 35 rounds, but was now a respectable blacksmith and a Winlaton bandsman.[138] Ridley used a minstrel tune written by Daniel Decatur Emmett in New York two years earlier, which was a favourite with the Confederates in the Civil War that had been raging since April.

THE BLAYDON KEELMAN.

AIR.—DIXEY'S LAND.

Oh lads aw's turned a keelman noo,
Wi' maw flannin drawers an' stockins blue,
On the Tyne, the Tyne, the Tyne, the Tyne.
In Blaydon aw was bred an' born
On the New Year's day at morn, on the Tyne, &c.

CHORUS :—Aw niver will leave Blaydon, ah ho! ah ho
For in Blaydon aw was bred an' born,
Aw niver will leave Blaydon, ah ho! ah ho the Blaydon lads for iver.

Noo there's Bob Chambers an' Harry Clasper,
Ne two in a boat thor can pull faster, on the Tyne, &c.
Then there's Winship an' awd Harry's son Jack,
These fower ageyn the world aw'll back, on the Tyne, &c.

We sailed fra' Blaydon wi' fire bricks loadin,
Smash aw believe maw fether's dotin', on the Tyne, &c.
For he ran agrund at Skinner's burn,
So we lost wor Tyne, an' had te lie till morn, on the Tyne, &c.

Thor's a new steamboat they call d the 'COWAN!'
For the Tyne commissioners ye'll find her towin, on the Tyne, &c.
She's always towin' ballast keels
Loaded wi' the big dredger doon at Sheels, on the Tyne, &c.

Noo aw've joined the Blaydon rifle corps,
Te guard wor canny Tyneside shore, on the Tyne, &c.
Wi' Airmstrang's guns we'll lick them bonny,
An' wor heed commander Coffee Johnny, on the Tyne, &c.

Noo maw wife leev'd servant at Blaydon burn,
Aw married her at Whickham church one morn, on the Tyne, &c.
In Robson Street we leeve tegither,
Aw work in the keel alang win her fether, on the Tyne, &c.

George Ridley's Local Song Book.

Early in November, the *Chronicle* reviewed Ridley's last night at the Tyne and noted, bizarrely, that the Gateshead 'vocalist and "poet"' sang 'Tyneside Songs' in the 'genuine Newcastle dialect'.

> Many of our local singers burlesque our singular but picturesque *patois*. But Mr. Ridley's songs are given with an ease and freedom from restraint that proves beyond doubt that he is a 'native' and 'to the manner born'. Several of his songs have reference to events that have occurred in Newcastle recently – 'Joey Jones' ... 'Harry Clasper, Chambers, Winship, and little Jack'; Mr. Stanley and his licence – all form themes to hang a string of verses on. The last one seems to be an especial favourite, each verse ending with a chorus (in which the audience joins) of 'three cheers for Stanley', and a declaration that of all the 'concerts in town there's nean can touch the Tyne'.

A week later, Stanley announced the 'Re-engagement of Mr. Geo. Ridley, the Tyneside Vocalist', who would 'sing a Selection of entirely new Compositions, written by himself'.[139]

John Wilson was born in 1792 in Petrie's Entry, next door to the Jack Tar pub on Sandgate Shore, Newcastle, and lived there all his life. His father made and mended cuckoo clocks, but 'Young Cuckoo Jack' became a waterman and hired out boats for sixpence an hour. He 'acquired the most intimate and unrivalled knowledge of the river', including 'the ebb and flow of its tides, its currents, bends, shoals, holes, sandbanks and other peculiarities'. He could pick up floating goods, and the dead and drowning, 'under almost any circumstances', 'with the most wonderful skill and dexterity', and 'was never known to fail when he was told where the person had fallen in and when'. He also picked up a 15-shilling fee from Newcastle Corporation for landing a corpse, but ten shillings for rescuing someone alive. He died on 2 December 1860, aged 68,[140] but tales about his 'tardiness to rescue the drowning and his alacrity to recover the dead' continued to circulate on Tyneside.[141] One man gave him a shilling for fishing him out of the river. '"Wey, hang thoo, " cried Jack, "aa wish aa'd lettin' thoo droon! Begox, aa wad hev gettin' ten bob at least for findin' thy body!"'[142]

In 1861, Ridley wrote a song about 'Cuckoo Jack', rowers and 'porter pokemen' – labourers who were 'all concert ganners' – but also included the recently deceased architect, Richard Grainger, and the industrialist, Sir William Armstrong. Ridley used a popular tune for *Newcastle Celebrities*, but his first publisher later altered his title.

NEWCASTLE ECCENTRICS.

AIR.—'NOTHING MORE.'

The day aw thowt aw'd hev a walk, aw wandered doon the quay.
Aw met Henwife Jack an' Ranter, they wor as drunk as they cud be;
They had just cum oot the Custum Hoose alang wi' fishwives mony a score
Shootin "buy maw caller herrin, hinny, an' aw'll ask for nothing more."

Awd Cuckoo Jack he's deed an' geyne, sum called him a knave.
He saved mony a muther's bairn fra' hevin a watery grave;
Deed bodies he got mony a one, just doon by the North Shore,
If ye paid Cuckoo for his labour, he wad ask for nothing more.

Dickey Grainger's hooked it te, he must hev been a strange creature,
Te build sic streets as Grey street an' sic a fine Theatre;
If they only had but let him leeve to the age of fowor score,
He wad finished Stephenson's monument, an' wad ask for nothing more.

There's Sir William Airmstrang, knighted by the Queen,
For makin' these guns for government, thor like was niver seen;
An' shud a foreign foe cum here te invade wor canny shore,
If we got the Airmstrang on we wad ask for nothing more.

Ye'll all knaw Harry Clasper, he's an honour te wor Tyne,
For pullin boats an' buildin them, he can all the rest ootshine;
Thor's Chambers, Winship, an' little Jack will join in a fower oar,
If we only mill the cocknies we'll ask for nothing more.

There's the porter pokemen that works upon the kee,
These is the cheps for jokin, an' they oft get on the spree,
They are all concert ganners, for singin they de adore,
Giv' them a fair day's wage an' fair day's wark an' they'll ask for nothing more.

George Ridley's Local Song Book.

Another song was also about local 'celebrities'.

Joseph Hogg of Gateshead and Joseph 'Tout' Forster of Swalwell, 'two of the most celebrated pedestrians the North ever produced', raced in Gateshead on 9 November, and the 'sensation' at Hogg's 'clever victory' was 'unequalled'.[143] Ridley used a US tune, *Kiss Me Quick and Go*, to celebrate his fellow townsman's victory.

HOGG AND FOSTER'S RACE.

AIR.—"KISS ME QUICK."

Tuther Seturday neet aw saw a grand foot race alang at the Victoria grund,
Between Tout Foster and Joe Hogg and the stake was fifty pnnd;
Thor was lots of cheps gettin on their bets, thor was little odds on Tout,
The cabs wor stannin at the gate, aw saw Joe Hogg luik oot·

CHORUS:—

Anaw says gan on Joe maw canny lad, thou hes a cliver style
Yell lick the Tout withoot a doot, this quarter of a mile.

The gate was opened, and sic a rush, thor was hundreds flockin in,
An' Jimmy Reay amang the crood says 'Hoggy's sure te win'
'Hoo can he loss' says Jimmy Dodds, 'the Ship will float the neet!'
Says Marky Hall 'we'll hev a rare blaw oot wi' tripe and and haggish meat.

The first iver Hoggy ran, it was wi' one the name o' Gilley,
Up at the Grapes for five aside, his backers drove him silly;
And aw mind he wun a handicap and a hurdle race likewise,
And at the Easter wrestlin, last year, he pull'd off the first prize.

He lick'd one o' the neym o' Miller twice, and Philipson in Newcassel;
And a deed heat he ran Geordy Wildbore, noo he there thor eyes did dazzel;
Then here's success te Hogg, Rowan, and White, and Belley te likewise,
Fra' ten miles tiv a quarter Gateshead can all the world surprise.

Noo Hoggy had a trainer bould, Tom Norvel was his neym,
They tuik their breethins at Primrose Hill, on the Friday neet cam' heym;
Man, Joe he luik'd vary fit, he seem'd te be runnin' fast,
And when he wun their Neddy sung "Joe we've put it on at last."

George Ridley's Local Song Book.

Ridley's main audiences were over in Newcastle, so he evidently hired cabs, and wrote a song about one Newcastle driver who specialised in taking sportsmen and punters to and from events. Ridley used the tune of a 'comic song'. In 1844, Henry Russell, the English-born anti-slavery and temperance campaigner in the USA, who was also a pianist and composer, had 'Arranged & Adapted a FAVORITE MELODY' for the Englishwoman Mary Howitt's 1829 poem, 'The Spider and the Fly'.[144] Vic Gammon believes that the melody was probably either *Mrs Bond* or *Will you come to the Bower*, and notes that Russell's piece was successful on both sides of the Atlantic.

THE CABMAN.

AIR.—"SPIDER AND THE FLY."

Oh cheps aw's turn'd a cabman noo, aw stand in St. Nicholas Square,
So if ye want te hire a one, yor sure te find me there,
Aw've a gud awd horse for gannin, he's a gudun up the banks
Ye see maw number's twenty-two, aw drive for Tommy Shanks

Chorus.—So if ye want te hire a cab, just call at St. Nicholas' Square,
Ye see maw number's twenty-two, yor sure te find me there.

If ye see me at Newcassel races just gi yorsel a treat,
Aw'll drive ye fra' the monument and away alang Blackett Street;
Aw flee past a' the uther cabs, not a minute will aw wait,
Aw shoot "cheps are ye gannin up? aw'll tip ye the winner of the plate."

Aw oft get a job at a bowling match, and sumtimes a foot-race,
That's ran at the Victoria grounds, smash man aw like that place;
'Cas de ye see aw haud the bets, aw gets sixpence te the pund,
Aw lends the cheps maw whup, ye knaw, te clear away the grund.

Ye shud see me aboot the hirin' time, when servants leave their place,
Aw's sure te get a job fra' them, aw've sic a winning face,
Aw puts thor boxes on the top; if she's a canny lass
She'll giv us a shilling for maw job and sixpence te get a glass.

Thor's two busses runs te Blaydon noo, and one up the Wind-
mill hills,
For a' thor opposishun us cabbys we leeve still;
And when aw gets a swell in drunk that leeves up West
Parade,
Aw charge him a bob when he gets in and swear he's niver
paid.

At funerals, weddins, or chrisnens, aw like sic jobs as these,
'Cas de ye see aw gets a rare blaw oot wi' rum an' breed an'
cheese,
And if aw get a weddin job which vary oft aw de,
Ye shud see me winkin' at the bride, then the bride she'll
wink at me.

George Ridley's Local Song Book.

Ridley's audiences evidently had few qualms about breaking the law if the victim was a well-to-do 'swell'.

Once again, Stanley applied at Manors Police Court for a three-month dramatic licence. For almost three months the Tyne 'had often been crowded to the doors', but 'the utmost good order had prevailed'. He focussed on 'vocal and instrumental music, and occasional performances of an acrobatic description', but wanted to 'present an entertainment of a higher and more intellectual nature', including 'works of our great dramatists' and the best 'works of modern dramatic literature'. The Theatre Royal proprietors and lessee did not object, but the magistrates refused to grant a licence. There were 'hisses' from Stanley's supporters,[145] and the *Chronicle* backed him.

Sidney Milnes Hawkes had trained as a barrister, but lost his fortune.[146] He was active in the plot to assassinate Louis Napoleon, and had taken Joseph Cowen junior's money to Mazzini and Garibaldi.[147] He now wrote a regular column in the *Chronicle*, as 'Elfin', and revealed that some magistrates had a financial reason for refusing Stanley's application. One had hinted that the North Eastern Railway Company, who owned the site, might 'pull down' the Tyne if it ever received a licence. Stanley advertised 'The Star Company of the North', 'licensed by Public opinion but not by the magistrates', in the *Chronicle*, which urged him to 'take the law into his own hands'.[148]

Late in November, a rower called Matfen raced Teasdale Wilson, the Sandgate keelman, on the Tyne.[149] Vic Gammon believes that Ridley used *The Whole Hog or None*, also known as *Old Hog or None*, for lyrics to celebrate the 'City' man's victory over the favourite.

TEASDALE WILSON, THE CITY CHAMPION.

Air—".The Happiest Man Alive."

Now ye've heard ov Teasdale Wilson,
He's a keelman doon the shore,
They call him the " City Champion,"
'Caws they nivor had one before.
For a Keel or in in Coble
He'll give ony man a race,
For five.and twenty pund aside
An' toss for choice of place.

CHORUS.

Now he's a Sandgit lad,
The bloomin' City Champion,
So lads noo get yor money on,
Ye may depend upon,
Wheniver he rows he always goes
The whole Hog or none.

Aw mind he rowed a coble race
Wi' Hopey doon at Blyth,
That race was for a hundred pund,
To win Hopey hard did strive ;
But the Sandgit cheps they shooted hard,
When the wind blew Teasdale about,
And the Porter-pokemen aw did say,—
He's the gamest lad that's out.

Chorus—Now he's a Sandgit lad, &c.

Aw mind when he rowed Matfid,
Now this agyen he won ;
Ye'd died a laffin' had ye been there
And ony seen the fun,
As Matfin he fell out of his boat
When he was two lengths forst,

When Teasdale turnd 'tis said,
He laffed till he nearly borst.

Chorus—Now he's a Sandgit lad, &c.

He licked little Dickey Clasper, tee,
This caused a great sensation,
'Twas two to one on Dick that day,
For that there was no 'casion ;
Mind Dickey took the lead at forst,
'An when they got to the shot tower,
Teasdale shut away a-heed,
Now isn't he a "Cure."

Chorus—Now he's a Sandgit lad, &c.

Aw can tell ye plenty mair he licked,
But aw think aw'l cut me stick,
They presented him wiv a watch and chain
An' aw hope to that he'll stick,
So lang many Teasdale florish,
An' to win he'll always strive,
The Sandgate cheps they all declare
He's the gamest lad alive.

Chorus—Now he's a Sandgit lad, &c.

George Ridley's New Local Song Book.

Ridley's focus on workers' leisure interests evidently remained successful, but Newcastle audiences were also able to see the 'Original Christy's Minstrels' from the USA.[150] The *Chronicle* noted that 'Mr. George Ridley' was 'well received every evening' at the Tyne and 'ably sustains his popularity'.[151] *The Era* reported that the company would perform at Harry Clasper's retirement testimonial.[152] The *Newcastle Courant* added that Stanley had offered his hall for the event and every artiste in town had volunteered to help.[153] The *Chronicle* stressed that Ridley's 'local songs' were 'a perennial source of amusement' at the Tyne and the 'popular vocalist' received 'no end of applause'. At the testimonial, 'The Tyneside Vocalist' would 'by particular desire, sing "Harry Clasper"' in 'the genuine vernacular'.

After the event, the *Chronicle* reported that Ridley 'sang with great success a local song', the 'words of which appeared a short time ago in our columns', and would appeal to 'all true Tynesiders'.[154] Vic Gammon believes that *Harry Clasper and His Testimonial* probably used the tune of *Gee Ho Dobbin*, as had the old local song, *Cappy*.

Times tries aw, they say, and they're not sae far rang,
Noo she's myed a tyuf trial, she's tested him lang—
Aw meen Harry Clasper, that weel chorised nyem,
For aw'm sure there's nee body can coupled wi' shyem.

Faithful awd Harry—plucky as ever
The still blooming poesy iv wor coaly river.

Times tried a' hor dodges, and says he's a' square,
Byeth in mind and in body—he's sound iverywhere;
Nee better man iver tyuek hawd iv an oar
Nor can she fynd fault wiv him when he's ashore.

Faultless aud Harry, &c.

Tyek him a' in a', as wise Shakesphere says,
(Aw've clean forgot where—but its in his plays),
Ye'll not fynd his equal in Tyems or in Tyne,
For in life or in death Harry Clasper 'll shine.

Matchless aud Harry, &c.

While larrel's are still hangin' thick roon'd his brow,
He's tyen in his heed for to bid ye adieu;
He thinks iv the young uns that are fond iv the skull.

And te ge them a chance he's ne mair gan to pull.
Thoughtful aud Harry, &c.

For the honors he's brought to wor canny Tyne,
Folks talk aboot givin' him somethin' that's fine—
A smart testimonial—an' aw think it's but fair,
For we can ye think that deserves a one mair ?
Canny aud Harry, &c.

Noo leuk what he's dyun' i' the boat-rowen way,
What fine skiffs he myed—ay, the besti' the day ;
An, leuk what a man he's trained intiv his place,
De ye think there's a chep dur row Chambers a race?
Wonderful Harry, &c.

Lets a' try wor best, and see if we can
Raise somethin' to say that we think him a man
That's chep iv respect : if to this ye agree,
To show ye are willin' join in chorus wi' me.
Worthy aud Harry, &c.

If we div'nt behave weel tiv him, ye see,
His ghost, when he's deed, 'ill be seen frae the kee
In a skiff, 'side the bridge, 'bout twelve iv'ry neet,
Till the mornin' cock craws, then he'll row oot iv seet.

Spirited Harry, the pride iv wor river,
Yor nyem it will flourish when ye're gyen for iver.

Thomas Allan, Tyneside Songs, 1862.

Yet it was not George Ridley who wrote the lyrics, but John Taylor, a 21-year-old clerk at Newcastle Central Station.

John Taylor.

Late in December, Stanley gave Newcastle magistrates a petition, signed by over 5,000 ratepayers, in support of his application for a dramatic licence, but they refused to grant one.[155]

The Era noted that 'Mr. G. Ridley (the Tyneside poet and singer)' was one of those who 'still maintain their *prestige* as first-class *artistes*' at the Tyne Concert Hall.[156] He needed new material. A fortnight earlier, a foot race had taken place at the Victoria Ground in Gateshead, and Ridley wrote a song, which he set to a popular old English tune, *Young Man from the Country*.

Ridley evidently had a particular affection for Blaydon.

BULLERWELL AND SUMMER'S RACE.

BY GEORGE RIDLEY.

Air.—"Young Man from the Country."

Aw'm gawn te tell ye aboot a race
That cum off som time back,
Bitween one Summers and Bullerwell,
This Summers was all thi crack,
Thi race was at thi Victoria grund,
They said Summers was gaun ti flee,
Says Bob aw cum frae Blaydon,
And ye'l not get ower me.

Noo when they both got at ti scratch,
Summer's backers they did chaff,
But Bob knawin' his little game
Did nowt but stand and laff,
When Bob's backers got thor money on
Summers wanted thi start d'ye see,
But says Bob aw cum frae Blaydon,
And ye'll not get ower me.

Noo off they went wi Bob in front,
Summer's backers went near mad,
They said that they could esely wun,
If he hadn't tyekin bad.
Noo away Bob went an' got the stakes,
And then they had a spree,
Says Bob aw'm frae the country,
An' ye'll not get ower me.

Noo away we gans ti the station,
And tyuk the half-past sevin train,
Then off we went ti Blaydon,

Ti the sign of the Rifleman,
An' there we all sat fuddlin',
We had a first-rate spree,
Says Bob aw cum frae Blaydon,
And ye'll not get ower me.

Then here's success to Bullerwell,
May he always be weel backed,
An' lang may Blaydon flourish,
Since they've pass'd the Local Act,
An' here's success ti the workin' man,
May he niver want a frind dy'e see,
So lads aw've sung ye aw maw song,
And ye'll get nee mair frae me.

Thomas Allan, Tyneside Songs, 1862.

Blaydon's Station Hotel around 1890.

5 *On the Road to Brighton*

In January 1862, George Ridley was the last remaining member of the Tyne Concert Hall company that he had joined over two months earlier; and, according to the *Chronicle*, he was writing 'a new local song', *Magistrates at the Concert*, to raise money to repair the Marlborough Street footpath. George Stanley presented two petitions to support his application for a dramatic licence, but the magistrates turned him down. The *Chronicle* reported that the 'really excellent professionals' in the Tyne's 'Christy Entertainment of the "Nigger Ball"' – an imitation of the Christy Minstrels – was competing successfully with the Theatre Royal pantomime, and would '"run" for some time', but Ridley would be 'as effective if he was not so demonstrative when he gave some of his Newcastle songs'.[157]

On 16 January 1862 a falling beam blocked the single shaft at Hartley Colliery in Northumberland and 204 men and boys died.[158] In February, Ridley was still one of the 'established favourites' at the Tyne,[159] and the Tyne company raised £21 for the Hartley fund,[160] donating a day's wages. After Ridley made his last appearance, Stanley announced an 'Entire Change of Company' and 'Great Novelties',[161] but Ridley evidently donated a further ten shillings to the fund.[162]

In March, the magistrates refused Stanley a licence yet again;[163] but in April Juliet Desborough gave dramatic readings at the Tyne. She also wrote to the *Chronicle*, claiming that the Theatre Royal manager had 'forcibly removed' her after a casting dispute, and 'Elfin' alleged that she had not received a fair share of the proceeds of her benefit night.

Supporters of the rower, Harry Clasper, had raised £200 to buy him a house, but needed another £150. The *Chronicle* announced that 'Through the liberality of Mr. Balmbra' there would be a 'Clasper Testimonial Concert' at the Wheat Sheaf Concert Room, and 'the Artists of this justly celebrated place of amusement' would perform. After the event, the *Chronicle* praised 'Mr. G. Ridley, the noted singer of Tyneside songs', for his performance. 'While the dialect is easily and naturally given, there is nothing coarse in the rendering of these songs, but they are such as the most refined audience might hear and be amused withal.' One was 'a ballad descriptive of a journey (in prospect) by road to the ensuing Blaydon races', which Ridley had 'adapted to a popular air'.

> A second song, containing some witty local allusions, was sung by the same vocalist, the principal portion of the ditty referring to the late contest between [John] Clasper and [George] Drewitt, in which the former was described as bent on going the whole animal for the 'two per cents', i.e. the £200 stakes.

(Ridley evidently used his favourite tune, *The Whole Hog or None*, but the lyrics have not been found.) The audience 'loudly applauded', but their appeals for an encore were 'not acceded to'.

Early in June, the *Chronicle* advertised a 'Grand Soirée and Ball' to celebrate the ninth anniversary of Whickham Mechanics' Institute. There was to be a 'Grand Concert', 'interspersed with Speeches and Songs, by Mr. George Ridley, of Gateshead, and others', in a 'spacious Marquee' in the Rectory grounds.[164] Parker's omnibus normally left the Wheat Sheaf in Newcastle for Blaydon at 1.40pm;[165] but on 9 June, omnibuses ran hourly from both the Cloth and Bigg Markets.

Next day, the *Chronicle* reported that the 'ancient village celebration' at Blaydon 'drew together a considerable concourse of people of all ages and both sexes, all attired in their holiday apparel'. There were the 'usual stalls for the sale of ginger-bread, nuts, "bullets, " and all other kinds of sweet things', which 'drove a large, and we hope (for the old ladies who presided over them) a profitable trade'. As for the crowds, the 'drenching rain destroyed all their pleasure in the afternoon', and evidently washed out the event in the Whickham Rectory grounds.[166] That evening, the 'musical and dramatic performance' in the Lecture Hall of the Mechanics' Institute in Tyne Street, Blaydon, was 'numerously attended'. Ridley 'acquitted himself' as Master of Ceremonies with 'considerable taste' and his 'local songs' received great applause.[167] He had added a new verse to a recent composition, [168] and sung it to the tune of *Brighton*.

BLAYDON RACES.

Air—"Brighton."

Aw went to Blaydon Races, 'twas on the ninth of Joon,
Eiteen hundred an' sixty-two, on a summer's efternoon,
Aw tuek the bus frae Balmbra's, an' she wis heavy laden,
Away we went alang Collingwood Street, that's on the
road to Blaydon.

CHORUS.

O lads, ye shud only seen us gannin,
We passed the folks upon the road just as they wor
stannin;
Thor wes lots o' lads an' lasses there, all wi' smiling faces
Gan alang the Scotswood Road, to see the Blaydon Races.

We flew past Airmstrang's factory, and up to the
"Robin Adair,"
Just gan doon te the railway bridge, the bus wheel
flew off there.
The lasses lost their crinolines off, an' the veils that hide
their faces,
An aw got two black eyes an' a broken nose in gan te
Blaydon Races Chorus—O lads, &c.

When we gat the wheel put on away we went agyen,
But them that had their noses broke, they cam' back ower hyem.
Sum went to the dispensary, an uthers to Doctor Gibb's,
An' sum sought out the Infirmary to mend their broken ribs. Chorus—O lads, &c.

Noo when we gat to Paradise thor wes bonny gam begun,
Thor wes fower-and-twenty on the bus, man, hoo they danced an' sung;
They called on me to sing a sang aw sung them "Paddy Fagan,"
Aw danced a jig an' swung my twig, that day aw went to Blaydon. Chorus—O lads, &c.

We flew across the Chain Bridge reet into Blaydon toon,
The bellman he was callin there—they call him Jackey Brown,
Aw saw him takin to some cheps, an' them he was pursuadin'
To gan an' see Geordy Ridley's concert in the Mechanics' Hall at Blaydon. Chorus—O lads, &c.

The rain it poor'd aw the day an' myed the groon'd quite muddy,
Coffy Johnny had a white hat on, they war shootin' "who stole the cuddy."

There wes spice-stalls an' munkey shows, an' aud wives selling ciders,
An' a chep wiv a happeny roond aboot shootin' now, me boys, for riders.
Chorus—O lads, ye shud only seen us gannin, &c.

George Ridley's New Local Song Book.

Ridley advertised John Balmbra's Wheat Sheaf, Parker's omnibus, William Armstrong's works, the Robin Adair pub in Benwell, the Infirmary on the Forth Banks, the Dispensary in Nelson Street and Dr. C.J. Gibb's surgery in Westgate Street, Newcastle, and, of course, 'Geordy Ridley's concert in the Mechanic's Hall at Blaydon'.

Armstrong's Elswick Works, 1870.

Scotswood Bridge around 1850.

Conrad Bladey found a minstrel tune called *Brighton* in *The Eclipse Self-Instructor for 5 string banjo: A complete instruction manual for playing banjo (using plectrum)*, published in the USA in the 1860s. In spite of its typical banjo figuration and different rhythms, Vic Gammon believes that this tune is very close to that of *Blaydon Races*.

Blaydon and Stella Mechanical Institute.

An old picture postcard of Blaydon, showing the racecourse.

However, it did not refer to the town in Sussex, but to its namesake in Massachusetts. Brighton, near Boston, was a good place for young men to sell cattle, hire a horse and wagon, get drunk, fight and get black eyes.[169] The lyrics of *On the Road to Brighton* varied considerably, as in *Canteen songster : a collection of the most popular songs of the day, comprising Sentimental, Comic, Negro, Irish, National, Patriotic, Social, Convivial, and Pathetic Songs, Ballads, and Melodies*, published in Philadelphia in 1866; but the

American Antiquarian Society's 'Ballad' dates from 1858 or 1859.[170]

In July, Ridley sang *Blaydon Races* at a West Ryton and Blaydon Mechanics' Institute Saturday Concert;[171] and the 'comic song' gave 'great gratification' to the workers at the Stella Coal Company's Towneley Colliery soirée.[172]

After the Newcastle magistrates rejected yet another application for a dramatic licence, 'Elfin' advised Stanley to 'take the law into his own hands'.[173] The Tyne closed for the summer, but he advertised for 'an ENTIRE COMPANY', including musicians who could play 'Cornet, Flute and Double Bass'.[174]

Late in August, the Tyne reopened with The Alabama Minstrels, the '*only Troupe* of Real Blacks in England'. Stanley re-engaged them until October, along with Mr. J. Moss, who had been a 'comic vocalist' at the 'Principal Music Halls'. The Tyne claimed to be the 'Star Company of the North' and had 'Vacancies for First-class talent only'.[175] Ridley was competing against national and international artistes; but the number of local celebrities was limited, and so was his repertoire of original 'local songs'.

According to a writer twenty years later, John Spencer was a 'well-known character' in Newcastle and 'extremely partial to changes'. Sometimes, he was a doorman at travelling exhibitions and drew 'a large audience' by describing 'the wonders within' with his 'fluent tongue' and 'unfailing wit'; but his behaviour could be 'wild and grotesque'.[176]

> He sold everything by turns and nothing long. Before 'lucky bags' were known, Jack struck out 'fresh fields and pastures new' in peddling. Strings of laces, cheap jewellery, clever new toys, whistles, little pistols, anything new or cheap Jack would hang upon his pole, and hawk about the streets. In broad humour, and untiring force of lung, he has in him the stuff to

make the ordinary Sheffield 'Cheap Jacks'. He is a fine sample of genius in humble life, thoroughly original in everything, and with a vividness that sends him headlong into all manner of eccentricities. Of oratory of the street type, Jack is a master; and should his flow of eloquence cease for a moment, a single word of banter from the crowd will suddenly bring him out again in all his glory. Of late years he has been more of a loose retainer to commerce than a merchant adventurer on his own account. He largely figures in doorways when goods are to be disposed of at a tremendous sacrifice; and his 'walk in ladies and gentlemen' was in a style which recalls the palmiest days of his street sales. As a descriptive talker Jack is unrivalled. He could spin a lecture an hour long out of a monkey's jaw bone, and possessed to the full the gift of amplification, which, let folks say what they please, has a great charm for the common people. One day he was in his glory. A wild beast show entered the town; and the train of caravans which slowly passed through the streets were closed by a 'real live' lion exhibited in his cage. To the rear of this caravan Jack manfully stuck, and whenever a halt took place his stentorian voice pealed over the heads of a mob of women and children – 'Ladies and gentlemen, this magnificent denizen of the desert now before you is generally known as –' but no pen could do justice to the tropical luxuriance of this speech.

Jack's wit was ready and his subtility caused much fun in a trial for assault in which he was charged with using a knife. When called upon for his defence he amazed everybody by declaring that he was 'Not guilty, ' for he emphatically declared – 'Gentlemen of the jury, it was not a knife I used, I assure you it was done with a fork.' Such it appeared was the case, and Jack like some other culprits was saved by that *bête noir* of lawyers – a 'flaw in the indictment'.

A well-known phrenologist was asked on a certain evening

> in the Lecture room to manipulate Jack's head; and the result was very amusing. No collusion was possible – Jack being suddenly brought in and sent forward to the platform. The energy, waywardness and talkativeness of our townsmen were hit off with surprising skill, and when thoughtfully regarding Jack's cranium, the lecturer said, 'You would make a good soldier now, but for obeying orders, I doubt you wouldn't do – you would always want to have your own way.' This statement elicited from Jack a smile of proud triumph, as he evidently regarded it as a tribute to his genius.[177]

What might have looked like eccentricity in 1882 did not necessarily correspond to how Newcastle people saw him in 1862.

Ridley wrote a song about Spencer, and borrowed a tune from a London-based concert hall artist. Sam Cowell had performed in the north east since at least 1857,[178] and had recently repopularised the tune of the smutty old song, *Bobbing Joan* for Theodore Hook's comic lyrics, which were roughly based on William Shakespeare's *Hamlet*.[179] (Vic Gammon notes that the tune is the same as *Rakes of Stoney Batter* and *Courting in the Kitchen*.) Ridley evidently assumed that his audiences would be familiar with some 'Cockney' terminology, and not be overly critical of a man who used to *nail* – steal – from *flats* – fools – or be shocked by knowing someone who occasionally spent a night in jail.

JOHN SPENCER.

BY G. RIDLEY.

Air—"Hamlet."

Maw name it is Jack Spencer,
Aw hawk aboot the toon,
Aw try ti keep yor sporrits up
When ye are lettin them gan doon
Aw'm not like the priests that preach,
And tells ye hoo te git ti heaven,
Aw patter hard yor hearts ti cheer,
And get mesel an honest livin.

Spoken—Back Combs, Side Combs, Ear Rings, Breast Pins, Steel Pens!

CHORUS.

Cock-a-doodle-dow, cock-a-doodle-doodle,
Cock-a-doodle-dow, cock-a-doodle-doodle.

Aw used ti try the peep-show dodge,
But that suin turned oot stale,
And then a quack doctor aw turned,
The flats aw used ti nail,
But one day a bobby he nailed me
For stannin in the street,
And ti the Manors he tuik me up,
And kept me there all neet.

Aw gets oot the next morning,
An' gans up ti Clayton street,
Aw call'd inti Young's, the sign o' the *Clock*
An' maw box was there all reet!
Aw there falls in wi' Adam Scott,
An' each of us had a glass o' whisky;
Adam danced a hornpipe fine,
Meesel, aw sung the Bay of Biscay!

The servant lass she says ti me—
"Aw say, John, d' ye want a wife?"
"No! no! says aw, d' ye think aw'm fond,
Or tired of maw life,—

Says aw, thor's mair get's married noo
Then what can manage te keep gud houses,
An' when we are working hard for brass,
Wi' yor nibors ye gan an' boozes."

Aw used ti follow a nice young lass,
She leev'd up Westgate Hill,
Aw used ti take her ower the moor
Ti see the rifles drill:

Oft ti Tynemouth, in her Sunday out,
Aw've seen us byeth sail doon the Tyne,
We'd cum up agyen wi' the eight train,
An' get her in tiv her place at nine.

So noo aw think aw'll cut me stick,
Aw've teld ye all what aw hev been,
An lang may Victoria leeve,
That is, ye knaw, wor canny Queen!
And lang may the soup kitchen stand
For ivery working man an' woman,

And lang may the soup kitchen stand
For ivery working man an' woman,
And aw hope it'll not be lang
Before we see the gud time cumin'.

Thomas Allan, Tyneside Songs, 1862.

Ridley was confident that his audiences would agree that 'ivery working man an' woman' would be grateful for charities like the Newcastle soup kitchen, and share his hope that everyone would 'see the gud time cumin', before too long.

Yet the Civil War in the USA, and the blockade of its Atlantic ports, had reduced the amount of Tyneside exports, and limited engineers' and other skilled workers' opportunities to earn spare cash through overtime, even if they still had a job. This, together with the national and international competition for engagements at larger halls, and Ridley's limited repertoire of original local material, undermined his chances of securing a regular income.

On 3 October 1862, the inauguration of a bronze statue of the famous Tyneside engineer George Stephenson, by Consett-born 64-year-old John Graham Lough, took place in Neville Street, near Newcastle Central Station.[180] Ridley wrote a song to celebrate the local heroes, but Vic Gammon believes that he used the tune, *Hey John Barleycorn*, not the English tune with a similar name.[181]

THE STEPHENSON MONUMENT.

Air.—"John-Barleycorn."

George Stephenson was as great a man
As any in the North;
Ye'll find his Monument stannin' now
In a place it's near the Forth:
He was a poor body's bairn,
And he used to drive a gin,
An' at neets he'd mend the nebors' shoes
His daily bread to win.

CHORUS.

Three cheers for Stephenson,
  George and Robert Stephenson,
Long may their names be heard
  On the Banks of Coaly Tyne.

George once got a Fireman's job,
  He had fourteen shilling a-week.
An' next he got a Brakesman's job,
  He then for a wife did seek;
He married one Fanny Henderson,
  Her fether was a working man,
An Robert he was ther only son,
  The cleverest in the land.
Chorus—Three cheers, &c.

Ye shud oney see thor little thach hoose,
  'Aside Wylam waggon-way,
The walls were plastered up wi clarts
  An' the flors war now't but clay.
There was three glass panes for windows,
  An' the rest war myed o' wood,
Now there stands a forst-rate beeldin'
  Where the aud thatch hoose once stood,
Chorus—Three cheers, &c.

The first locomotive that he myed,
  The "Rocket" she was ca'd,
He said she'd run ten miles an hour,
  The fokes thow't he'd gyen mad.
These days there was ne iron rails,
  The waggon-ways were wood,
He said she'd run as hard agyn,
  And they said she never could.

Chorus—Three cheers, &c.

Now George he suen left Newburn
  For he knew he was reet clivor;
He shifted doon to Willington Quay
  That's ten miles doon the river.
He invented a steam ballast crane,
  Which got him a greet nyem.
The aud ballast crane is stannin' yet
  At least aw'm told the syem.

Chorus—Three cheers, &c.

Now ye see how clivor a man may be,
  Tho' he's brought up verv poor,
And Robert he was as clivor a man
  As ivor thor lived aw'm sure ;
Now think on what aw've telled ye, lads,
  An' always keep't in min'
An' try to be a Stephenson,
  Two o' the cliverest men o' Tyne.

George Ridley's New Local Song Book.

The unveiling of the Stephenson memorial, 1862.

Since Ridley was unsure whether Stephenson's crane was still working, ten miles downriver from Gateshead, he evidently did not travel very far, but he was not the only one who had found making a living as a full-time entertainer rather difficult.

John Sessford, Balmbra' former pianist, was now a 'Watchmaker', and lived at 3 St Martin's Court, off Newgate, with his wife, Mary, a 16-year-old son who was an 'Engine Wright', and four girls, aged seven to 14. Balmbra's lead violinist, Charles Easthope, a 'Professor of Music', and his wife, a 16-year-old daughter who was a 'Dressmaker', and two boys, aged eight and four, shared the Sessford's accommodation. In October, John Sessford cut his throat with a razor, reportedly on account of 'family troubles', and died days later.[182]

Ridley performed at 'many a country mechanics' soiree and social festival', [183] but he needed to supplement an irregular income.

George Stephenson.

6 *George Ridley's Local Song Book*

Ralph Allan was born in Edmonton, Scotland, in 1802, and Alice McDougal in 'Brigham' – probably Birgham in Berwickshire – around 1806. On 25 March 1828, they married in St Mary's Church, Gateshead. Seven months later, on 29 December, Ralph junior was baptised at the United Secession Presbyterian Chapel, Carliol Square, Newcastle, and on 11 October 1830, so was his sister Elizabeth.[184] The Allans' third child, Thomas, recalled:

> I was born in 'Pitman's Row', Forth Banks, November 25th 1832, the year the Cholera first appeared in England. When a boy I recalled my mother speaking of it and telling me of the dread it inspired.
>
> My father was a blacksmith working at Usher's coach works, Forth Banks, and made the iron work for a sort of hearse which the authorities sent daily around to gather up the dead during the raging of the disease.[185]

Robert and Launcelot Usher were old-established coachbuilders,[186] and sold second-hand 'chariots' and 'phaetons' to the wealthy.[187]

George Allan was born on 30 March 1835, but was baptised at St John's Church in Newcastle, as was Robert on 5 September 1838.[188] By 1841, Ralph Allan, a 'Spring Maker', Alice, and five children lived in Forth Street. Nicholas was born on 17 September. William followed on 9 April 1844. According to Thomas's grandson, Maurice, Nicholas was 'a little lacking in brain', and someone erased the place of his and William's christenings from the family Bible.[189]

Ralph Allan senior did not have a vote,[190] and, like the other children, Thomas was 'brought up a radical'.[191] He probably went to St John's Charity School in Cross Street, off Westgate Street, which had taught 44 'poor boys' since 1705. They each received a pair of shoes and stockings at Christmas, and another pair of shoes and stockings, a blue coat, cap, waistcoat, leather breeches, shirts and bands at Midsummer. Some craft guilds had recently stopped making the donations to guarantee their sons a place, and other parents who paid £3 a year could secure one.[192] Thomas recalled:

> At school I was a fair scholar, at least in reading and writing, but arithmetic I never could grapple with.
>
> The schoolboy's rhyme of the time was true in my case
>
> 'Multiplication is vexation,
> Division is as bad,
> The 'Rule of Three' puzzles me
> And 'Fractions' makes me mad.'
>
> As showing the difference in boys, I had a companion, William Lisle. While I was struggling with to me a puzzling question he simply seemed to do it without an effort. He had a gift for figures. I had none, and do what he would (he lived beside me and we went to and came from school together) he could not learn me.[193]

When boys became apprentices, they received £2, a Bible, a Prayer Book and an Anglican devotional work, *The Whole Duty of Man*.[194]

Probably in 1846, when Thomas was 14, he was apprenticed to Christopher Rutter, a blacksmith and coachbuilder, whose workshop was next door to Robert and William Hawthorn's Engine Works on Forth Banks.[195]

'Hawthorns' cheps' and boys worked 60 hours a week and

were paid time and a half for overtime. They were fined for breaking the 'Rules and Regulations', but the money went into an 'Accident and Sick Fund' and all the employees shared anything that remained at the end of the year. Because of the railway-building boom, the workforce almost had doubled to over 1,000 between 1844 and 1847,[196] and they needed larger premises, so Hawthorn's bought Rutter's workshop, employed him as a foreman, and accepted Thomas as an apprentice.[197] He recalled:

> Workmen's trips ... were unknown until about 1847, when R. & W. Hawthorn begun them by giving the workmen at their famous engine works, Forth Banks, a two-day trip to Edinburgh. It being the first of its kind (the factory band accompanying it), the trip made a great talk, and St Nicholas' bells were rung in honour of the occasion.[198]

The *Newcastle Courant* reported that on Friday 'about a thousand' of Hawthorn's 'mechanics' travelled on the Newcastle and Berwick and North British Railways to Edinburgh, and 'met those belonging to the Leith establishment, in number about eight hundred (who previously came up by the Edinburgh, Leith, and Granton Railway) at the termini, about two o'clock'.

> After being marshalled in procession, they paraded the city for some time, accompanied by bands of music. Many of the party carried numerous mechanical devices, and party coloured ensigns, on which were inscribed a number of appropriate mottoes. After having satisfied themselves with this display, the party broke up and retired to the Large Waterloo Rooms, where refreshment was provided for them, while the principal individuals sat down to dinner at the Waterloo Hotel. The greater portion of the Newcastle party returned on Saturday, and arrived at their homes about midnight.[199]

The Newcastle pub fiddler and singer Bobby Nunn wrote a lengthy song about the journey and the 'sights', and, thanks to Thomas Allan, a fragment survives.[200]

In 1851, Ralph and Alice Allan lived in Ridley Court, 91 South Street, close to Robert Stephenson's locomotive works, and not far from Forth Banks. Elizabeth had no outside occupation, but Ralph junior was an 'Engine Smith', as were Thomas and George. Robert was a 'Scholar', and so were Nicholas and William.

Hawthorns' works now built locomotives and employed around 900 men and boys. Single young engineers, living with their parents, could save from their relatively high wages,[201] and by the mid-1850s Ralph Allan junior had opened a stationer's shop in North Shields. Thomas stayed at Hawthorns',[202] but he 'did not enjoy robust health';[203] and by 1858 he had enough capital to set up as a newsagent and stationer at 8 Collingwood Street, Newcastle, and live at 51 George Street, off Westgate Street.

By 1861, Ralph and Alice Allan may have died. Ralph junior, a 'Stationer & Bookseller' at 1 Church Way, was living in rooms at 11 Camden Street, North Shields, with his 31-year-old wife, Ann, born in Walbottle, Northumberland. Their son Ralph was five and James was two.

Thomas Allan had a second shop in Dean Street, Newcastle.[204] He had a 'great love' for reading, and a keen interest in local celebrities and in listening to orators and singers.[205] On 10 November, he wrote a contract, with a sixpenny stamp to make it legally binding. The witness, Thomas Gregson, was a former Chartist, and his watchmaker's shop was next door to Allan's in Collingwood Street.

Allan published an eight-page songbook.

Joseph Davis had moved from Mosley Street a year earlier,

I George Ridley Author and sole owner of the following songs hereby sell them to Thomas Allan Bookseller & Collingwood St. Newcastle on Tyne & giving up all rights to the songs

Johnny Luck Up the Bellman
The Bobby Cure
The Cabman
John Spencer
Hogg & Foster Race
The Blaydon Keelman
Joey Jones
Bullerwell & Summers Race
Newcastle Celebrities
The Rifleman

Signed Thomas Allan

Newcastle on Tyne Nov 11/62 George Ridley
Witness Thomas Gregson

Thomas Allan, 'Agreement with G. Ridley'.

and was also an engraver,[206] but it seems unlikely that he made the woodcut of Ridley, dressed for *The Bobby Cure*. Allan did not include *Bullerwell and Summers Race* or *John*

Spencer, but he renamed *Newcastle Celebrities* as *Newcastle Eccentrics*. He was now a wholesaler, and this penny 'COPYRIGHT' publication had 'a large sale'.[207]

Allan was publishing 16-page penny 'numbers' of *Tyneside Songs* by various writers. Joe Wilson, who later became a famous 'local' singer-songwriter, set the type for the printer, Mr Beal,[208] and some of Ridley's pieces appeared in the second 'number'. Its first page pictured him dressed as John Higgins, the former Gateshead Bellman, with a ragged waif holding his coat.

No. 1.--COPYRIGHT.--PRICE 1d.

GEORGE RIDLEY'S

LOCAL SONG BOOK.

THE GATESHEAD POET.

GEORGE RIDLEY'S SONGS.

[THE BOBBY CURE.]

Written and Sung by him, with great applause, at the Newcastle Concerts, upwards of 150 Nights.

CONTENTS:

THE BOBBY CURE.
JOHNNY LUIK UP.
NEWCASTLE ECCENTRICS.
THE RIFLEMEN.
THE CABMAN.
HOGG & FOSTER'S RACE.
JOEY JONES.
BLAYDON KEELMAN.

Newcastle-on-Tyne:
Published by THOMAS ALLAN, Bookseller and News Agent, 8, Collingwood Street and 45, Dean Street.
Song Books in great variety. The Trade Supplied.
Printed by J. Davis, Printer, 50, Grainger Street.

All the ten Ridley songs appeared in this and later numbers, but Allan changed *The Riflemen* to *The Rifleman* and subtitled *John Spencer* with '*All Aboard for a Penny*'.[209]

Mr. George Ridley as "Johnny Luik up"
In his celebrated Song of that name, sung by him upwards of 300 nights at the Newcastle Concerts.

Thomas Allan, Tyneside Songs, 1862.

Ridley had not sold his most recent pieces, *Teasdale Wilson*, *Blaydon Races* and *The Stephenson Monument*; but he still needed new material. He sympathised with 'young cheps' looking for wives, and probably around this time, he wrote a 'song of songs'.

THE SHEELS LASS FOR ME.

Air—"The whole hog or none."

The uther day we went to Tinmuth,
  Some mair young cheps and me,
An' the first place that we called in,
  Was the "Cottage by the Sea."
There was a young lass sitting,
  They called her "Nancy Till,"
She was axin' "Aud Bob Ridley"
  To gan an' hev a gill.

CHORUS.

Oh, ye lasses all, the truth aw'll tell ye hinny,
Tyneside's the place where the lasses are se bonny,
    An' if ever aw get married
    There's a Sheels lass for me.

Now in cum "Billy Pattison"
  Alang wi "Minnie Clyde,"
He said, just "Wait for the Waggon"
  An' ye'll all get a ride.
Then in cum "Annie Laurie"
  Alang wi' "Robin Grey,"
The "Jolly Waggoner" brought in "Doran's Ass"
  To tyek the waggon eway.
        Chorus—Oh, ye lasses all, &c.

Then in comes "Peter Gray"
  Wi' "Rosalie, the Prairee Flower,"
An' the "Young Man from the Country"
  Alang wi' the "Perfect Cure,"
Next in comes "Nelly Grey,"

And "Widow Machree" was cryin'—
  Oh! "'Tis hard to give the Hand."
        Chorus—Oh, ye lasses all, &c.

Then in cum the "Artful Dodger,"
  He was on the "Low Back'd Car,"
He was gan ti "Limerick Races"
  Wi' "Pat of Mullingar."
Then in comes "Gentle Annie."

She was singin' "Ole King Cole,"
"Pat Murphy" he was there tee,
Just come from the "Old Bog Hole."
Chorus—Oh, ye lasses all, &c.

The "Young Man from the Country"
Was sittin on the floor,
He said if he'd a "Ragged Coat"
He'd "Ask for Nothing More."
"There is a Flower that Bloometh,"
'Tis the "Last Rose of Summer,"
"Ben Bolt" cried from the "Old Arm Chair"—
"What's a' the Steer, Kimmcr."
Chorus—Oh, ye lasses all, &c.

The next aw saw "John Barleycorn,"
He was there wi' "Nelly Bly,"
She sung "My own my Guiding Star"
And "No Irish need Apply."
Now it was "So early in the Morning,"
That we heard the "Postman's Knock,"
Then we all sung "God Save the Queen,"
An' the company up was broke.
Chorus—Oh, ye lasses all, &c.

George Ridley's New Local Song Book.

One tune was new. Allan recalled that *No Irish Need Apply* was a response 'to the offensive ending of many advertisements' for work. He thought that Ned Corvan had written its lyrics;[210] but they evidently originated in London and crossed the Atlantic to the USA, where John F. Poole's rendition became highly successful.[211]

Because of the blockades at US Atlantic ports, Lancashire weavers lacked raw cotton. In November, Emilie Stanley, George's wife, died leaving five children, including one who was nine months old.[212] Stanley applied for permission to organise a benefit for the Lancashire Distress Fund, but the magistrates refused.[213] Joseph Cowen junior had been elected unopposed to Newcastle town council,[214] and the *Chronicle* publicised the bench's callous decision.[215]

Probably in time for Christmas, Thomas Allan bound six 'numbers' of *Tyneside Songs* as a 'Second Edition' and named Corvan and Ridley on the title page. No individual 'numbers' survive, but each of the 16-page sections had a serial number and an illustration on the first page. The book probably cost sixpence, [216] and was the first large collection of 'local' songs since Joseph Philip Robson's *Songs of the Bards of the Tyne* of 13 years earlier.

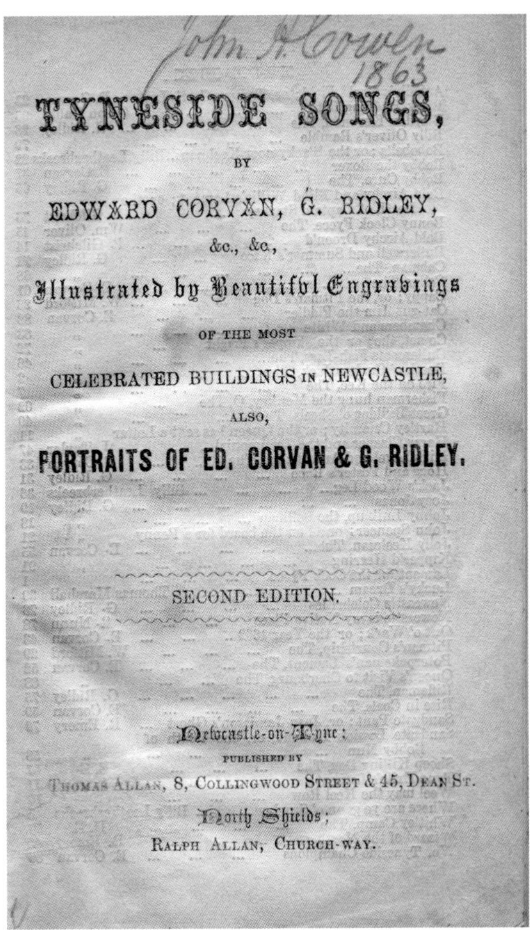

TYNESIDE SONGS,

BY

EDWARD CORVAN, G. RIDLEY,

&c., &c.,

Illustrated by Beautifvl Engravings

OF THE MOST

CELEBRATED BUILDINGS IN NEWCASTLE,

ALSO,

PORTRAITS OF ED. CORVAN & G. RIDLEY.

SECOND EDITION.

Newcastle-on-Tyne:

PUBLISHED BY

THOMAS ALLAN, 8, COLLINGWOOD STREET & 45, DEAN ST.

North Shields;

RALPH ALLAN, CHURCH-WAY.

Thomas Allan, Tyneside Songs, 1862.

7 *George Ridley's New Local Song Book*

By 1863, George Stanley lived at 18 Ashfield Terrace, Newcastle.[217] He advertised in *The Era* for 'First-class TALENT' for the Tyne Concert Hall, including a 'Comic Vocalist', and was ready to negotiate with a circus proprietor to open on Easter Monday.[218] In April, he engaged a 'celebrated equestrian troupe' and 'rearranged' the interior as 'an admirably fitted up circus'.[219]

Twenty-three-year-old James T. Tute from Macclesfield was a 'double-handed Musician (Violin and Cornet)' and 'Leader of the Band' at the Tyne. In June, he advertised in *The Era* for the post of '*chef d'orchestre*' elsewhere, since the Tyne was closing for the 'Summer Season' at the end of the month, and he requested that written offers should go to Stanley.

In July, the Tyne was 'closed for Extensive Alterations', but Stanley required 'Talents and Novelties' for the re-opening. By August, the interior of the building was 'completely remodelled and altered'.

> [T]he promenade has been extended the full length of the auditorium, the boxes raised, beautifully ornamented and cushioned, and the pit carried underneath the promenade and boxes. The stage has been considerably enlarged and a new proscenium fitted up; the whole lighted up with a very handsome chandelier; the orchestra has also been considerably enlarged and augmented, and is under the leadership of Mr. Derbyshire.

On the opening night the Hall was 'well filled' and 'the whole of the artistes engaged were most favourably received'.[220] Twenty-three-year-old Joseph Watson Derbyshire, 'a very fine violinist', had once been a musical landlord.[221]

Robert Chambers had beaten Richard Green of Australia in a boat race on the Thames to become the world champion, [222] and Ridley celebrated his victory, using the same tune as he had for other lyrics about Tyneside rowing champions.

CHAMBERS.

Air—"The whole hog or none."

Now, lads, ye've heerd of Chambers,
He's bet the Asstrilyen Green,
For pullin a skiff there is ne doot
He's the best ther's ivor been.
He has regular locomotiv' speed,
He's upreet, honest, and true,
Wheniver he pulls wiv a pair ov sculls
Aw puts on ivory screw!

CHORUS.

Oh, ye Cockneys all,
Ye mun think't very funny,
For Bob he gans an licks ye all
An collars all aw yor money,
Whenivor he rows, he always goes,
The whole hog or none.

Aw hear when Bob was nine year aud
He oft played the wag frae skuil;
He oft wad steel a boat away
An gan an hev a pull.
Hee's fether often tanned hees hide,
But Bob he didn't care,
Now, fether, he says, if ye dinnat bray's
Am sure aw'l did ne mair.

Chorus—Oh, ye Cockneys all, &c.

Bob struggled hard fra been a bairn
Fore he got to what hee's now,
He puddled iv Walker Rowlin Mill
But he's pull'd heessel safe throu';
An aw hope each job he tyeks in hand
Hee'l always hev fair play.

An think a number one—that is—
  Never give a chance away,
        Chorus—Oh, ye Cockneys all, &c,

Now when Bob and Green they pulled thor match,
  This Green luik'd very wild,
He tuik the lead of Bob at forst
  Till they got abyun a mile.
But Harry gov Bob the office then,
  Saying aw'l lay ten to ite,
The Reporter of the "Chronicle" said
  That Greeny then turned white.
        Chorus—Oh, ye Cockneys all, &c.

Now Bob hee's licked byeth Green and White,
  And Kelly, an' Everson an aw,
An Cooper put the Mackey on,
  And stopped the Cockney's craw.
This Green wad fain row Bob agyn,
  But aud Harry he wants a bigger stake,
They munna think to catch him asleep
  For he's always wide awake.
        Chorus—O ye Cockneys all, &c.

Tyck Bob all in all, as Shakespere says,
  We'll neer see his like agyen,
He waddant de an unjust thing
  To hurt poor working men;
Win if he can, it is his plan,
  So get yor money on,
For whenivor he shows he always goes
  The whole Hog or none.
        Chorus—O, ye Cockneys all, &c.

George Ridley's New Local Song Book.

Ridley testified to Chambers' honesty, because he would not throw a race, but he also gave Cowen's *Chronicle* a plug.

In October, the 'favourite local singer' and 'Gateshead poet' topped the bill at the Tyne Concert Hall for five nights and had a benefit on the sixth.[223] Stanley doggedly applied for a dramatic licence. He pointed out that over the past two years 'many thousands of people of all classes' had visited the Tyne, but there had never been 'any cause for complaint on the ground of disorder or irregularity'.[224] It was a circus in summer and a 'Concert-room' in winter.

> The entertainments ... are, and always have been, unobjectionable, on the score of morals; all expressions and performances that can offend the tastes of the most fastidious are scrupulously avoided ... [and] it is my wish to make my Hall a place of resort where the audiences can not only be amused but also instructed; to afford the working classes, in fact, a place of pleasant and intellectual recreation free from the temptations which the sale of intoxicating drinks always offer.

The magistrates hinted that it would be 'most desirable that if a second Theatre is to be established' it 'should be one of a permanent character',[225] but refused a licence.[226] That night, Stanley announced from the Tyne stage that he would open a new permanent theatre.[227]

Ridley sold the copyright of five more songs to Thomas Allan, who published another 'COPYRIGHT' penny songbook.

George Ridley's New Local Song Book.

Allan retitled *Chambers* as *Bob Chambers* on the front page and added two older 'local' pieces that Ridley may have performed. He acknowledged William Oliver, the singing grocer who died in 1848, as the author of *Newcastle Props*, but did not credit Bobby Nunn, the blind fiddler who died in 1853, for *Blind Willie's Deeth*. On the back page, Ridley sought engagements at small venues.

'GEORGE RIDLEY',

Gateshead Poet and Vocalist.

The most successful delineator of the day of Local, Irish, Comic, and Sentimental Songs, respectfully informs the Directors of Mechanics' Institutes, the Managers of Soirees, and the Promoters of all Social Gatherings, that he is at liberty to attend all meetings of a social character, and sing, amongst others, his own celebrated Songs, "Johnny Luik up," the "Bobby Cure," as sung by him upwards of 300 Nights at the Newcastle Concerts.

Address—GEORGE RIDLEY, No. 1, Grahamsley Street, Gateshead.

Inquiries may also be made of T. Allan, Bookseller, 16, Collingwood Street.

He had his photograph taken, possibly for a business card.

Allan's Illustrated Edition of Tyneside Songs, 1891.

Ridley wore a collar, tie and smart jacket, and slicked his hair with oil to form a neat parting. He had a well-scrubbed face; but it looked rather thin, tight-lipped, hollow-cheeked and sunken-eyed for someone who was only 28.

Early in 1864, the *Newcastle Daily Journal* reported about an experimental time gun.[228] Ridley needed to add to his modest repertoire of original material, and wrote *The Time Gun*, [229] but the lyrics have not been traced.

He faced stiff competition, especially at the larger Tyneside venues, from London-based singer-songwriters like Harry Clifton, whose recent comic hit, *Pretty Polly Perkins*, described a Cockney milkman's sourness, sexual naiveté and failure to establish a relationship with a woman. Ridley used Clifton's tune and theme; but his 'keelman' had been close enough to the woman he loves to know the colour of her bed gown and stockings. He also knew her cousin, Tom Gray, the 'muckman' – one of the men employed by the local authority to shovel excrement from unflushable domestic toilets – and about her affair with a hewer from his own former workplace, Shipcote Colliery.

CUSHEY BUTTERFIELD.

Air—"Polly Perkins."

THE LAST SONG WRITTEN BY GEORGE RIDLEY.

Aw's a broken-hearted keelman, an' aw's owerheed in luv
Wiv a yung lass in Gyetshead, an' aw calls her me duv;
Her nyem's Cushy Butterfield, an' she sells yalla clay,
An' her cusin is a muckman, an' they call him Tom Gray.

KORUS.

She's a big lass an' a bonny one,
An' she likes her beer;
An, they call her Cushy Butterfield,
An' aw wish she was here.

Her eyes are like two holes in a blanket burnt throo,
An' her brows in a mornin wad spyen a yung coo;
An' when aw heer her shootin "Will ye buy ony clay,"
Like a candy man's trumpet, it steels maw young hart
away.

KORUS—She's a big lass, an' a bonny one, &c.

Ye'll oft see hor doon at Sandgate when the fresh herrin
cums in ;
She's like a bagfull o' sawdust tied roond wiv a string ;
She weers big golashes, te, an' her stockins was wonce
white,
An' her bedgoon is a laelock, an' her hats nivor strite.
KORUS—She's a big lass, an' a bonny one, &c.

When aw axed her te marry me, she started te laff,
" Noo, nyen o' yor munkey tricks, for aw like ne such
chaff !"
Then she start'd a bubblin, an' she roar'd like a bull,
An' the cheps i' the keel says aw'm nowt but a fyeul.
KORUS—She's a big lass, an' a bonny one. &c.

She says, " The chep that gets me 'll heh te work ivry
day, [seek clay ;
An' when he cums hyem at neets he'll heh te gan an
An' when he's away seekin 't, aw'll myek balls an' sing,
" Weel may the keel row that maw laddie's in !"
KORUS—She's a big lass, an' a bonny one, &c.

Noo, aw heer she hes anuther chep, an' he hews at
Shipcote, [throat ;
If aw thowt she wad deceeve me, aw'd sure cut me
Aw'll doon the river sailin, an' sing " Aw'm afloat,"
Biddin adoo te Cushey Butterfield an' the chep at
Shipcote.
KORUS—She's a big lass, an' a bonny one, &c.

Thomas Allan, A Choice Collection of Tyneside Songs, 1872.

Allan later claimed that a 'big' 'Gyetside lass' called 'Cushey Butterfield' protested to 'Geordie' Ridley 'ageyn bein' myed a sang on', and threatened to 'give him a cloot o' the jaws for his impiddence'. The songwriter 'got over the difficulty by asserting that the name was not meant for anyone in particular',[230] but the lyrics were not published immediately. Allan may have found Ridley some engagements, but the singer had a friend in an influential position.

Early in 1862, Tom Handford had completed his third

engagement at the Tyne Concert Hall. By autumn 1863, 'Handford's People's Concerts' were 'pleasing large audiences in his considerably-improved Hall' in Sans Street, Sunderland,[231] and by December he managed Balmbra's in Newcastle.[232] In January 1864, Handford ran 'People's Concerts' there, but he also performed at the Victoria Music Hall and Barlow's Circus Royal.[233]

George Stanley married 18-year-old Frances from near Consett, in St Nicholas's Church, Newcastle. In February, the son of Handford's billposter spotted John Ritchie, Stanley's billposter, tearing down Handford's bills in Neville Street.[234] Handford summonsed Ritchie and testified that he had 'an exclusive right from Mr Young, sculptor, to put bills on that wall' and it would be a 'great inconvenience' to 'post them up again'. The magistrates fined Ritchie two shillings and sixpence, plus costs, and 'desired that any rivalry between the two music saloons and their bill-stickers should cease'.[235]

In April, there were 'Crowded houses nightly' at Handford's Music Hall for 'George Ridley (The Tyneside Poet)';[236] but according to Allan, 'In the midst of this success after a short public career of about 5 Years' – in fact he had been a full-time professional for less than three – Ridley's health 'began seriously to fail'.[237]

In June, John Balmbra put the Wheat Sheaf up for sale. In July, at a 'grand concert' in the Lecture Room, Nelson Street, Bob Chambers showed his rowing trophies and Handford and other artistes performed 'for the benefit of Mr. G. Ridley', who was 'lying ill', and 'unable to follow his profession'.[238] His illness 'rapidly began to assume a dangerous appearance', and he died at 1 Grahamsley Street, Gateshead, on 9 September.[239] Next day, his mother Frances put her cross on the death certificate, which gave the age of the 'Vocalist' as 30, though he was still 29.

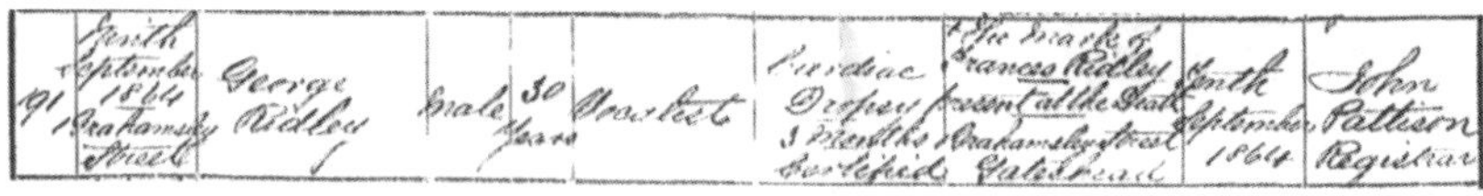

91	Tenth September 1864 Grahamsley Street	George Ridley	male	30 years	Vocalist	Cardiac Dropsy 3 Months Certified	The mark of Frances Ridley present at the Death Grahamsley Street Gateshead	Tenth September 1864	John Pattison Registrar

George Ridley's death certificate.

Symptoms of 'Cardiac dropsy' include abnormal amounts of fluid in the spaces between the cells of the body, as a result of heart disease, caused by the obstruction of blood in the heart, lungs or liver.

On 11 September, a 'large number of his friends and admirers' followed Ridley's coffin to the new Gateshead East Cemetery,[240] and Reverend William Bennett of Holy Trinity Church recorded the burial.

George Ridley	Grahamsley Street	September 11th	30 years	W. Bennett Incl of Trinity
No. 21.				

George Ridley's burial record (courtesy of Peter Jefferies).

Once again, Ridley's age was incorrect.

Next day, 'Elfin' wrote a touching obituary in the *Chronicle*, and put Ridley's age as 'about 30'.

> Poor George Ridley, the well-known local singer, is dead. He has been long ill, and unable to follow his employment, and he gradually sunk and died on Friday afternoon. He was well-known in this district, and his presence will be missed at many a country mechanics' soiree and social festival. Ridley was a labourer, and when engaged tipping the wagons at Hawks, Crawshay, and Sons works some years ago, he got himself severely crushed. This accident prevented him engaging in any manual labour again, and having a good voice and taste for singing, he took to the vocation of a vocalist as a means of getting a livelihood. His popularity with the people was

> considerable, and he had repeated engagements in all the concert halls in the district. He was only about 30 years of age, and unmarried. Personally he was a very decent man, and his death will be regretted by a large circle of friends.[241]

There was no obituary in the *Newcastle Courant*, *Newcastle Guardian* or *Gateshead Observer*.

The ‘Third Edition’ of Thomas Allan’s *Tyneside Songs* probably appeared in time for Christmas. The title page and Index appear to have survived, but the 96-page book contained the same ten Ridley songs as the ‘Second Edition’ and on the same pages.[242] Allan had evidently continued to sell the 16-page ‘numbers’ separately. Once again, only Corvan’s and Ridley’s names appeared on the title page.

Thomas Allan reportedly published Ridley’s *The Time Gun* and *Broken Hearted Keelman* as single-sheet slip songs,[243] but neither has been traced.

TYNESIDE SONGS,

BY

EDWARD CORVAN, G. RIDLEY,

&c., &c.,

Illustrated by Beautiful Engravings

OF THE MOST

CELEBRATED BUILDINGS IN NEWCASTLE,

ALSO

PORTRAITS OF ED. CORVAN & G. RIDLEY.

THIRD EDITION.

Newcastle-on-Tyne:

PUBLISHED BY

THOMAS ALLAN, 16, COLLINGWOOD ST., AND 62, DEAN ST.

North Shields:

RALPH ALLAN, TYNE STREET.

Thomas Allan, Tyneside Songs, 1864.

8 *A Choice Collection of Tyneside Songs*

By 1865, Thomas and George Allan lived at 45 Dean Street, Newcastle,[244] and ran a shop at 62 Dean Street, on the corner of Mosley Street. Thomas Fordyce's 'Printing Office' was upstairs.

In July, 65-year-old Joseph Cowen senior became a Newcastle MP,[245] and Ned Corvan died in September, aged 37.[246]

Probably in time for Christmas, and without mentioning George, Thomas and Ralph Allan put the dead songwriters Corvan and Ridley first and second on the title page of a larger edition of their songbook, and two older living songwriters third and fourth.

62 Dean Street (Allan Papers).

The six 16-page 'numbers' with ten Ridley Songs were the same as in *Tyneside Songs*, and were bound with six 14-page sections, [247] and Thomas Allan's 1863 *Popular Guide* to Newcastle.

Author's collection

A
CHOICE COLLECTION
OF
TYNESIDE SONGS,
BY
E. CORVAN, G. RIDLEY, J. P. ROBSON,
R. EMERY, &c., &c., &c., &c., &c.,
ILLUSTRATED BY
BEAUTIFUL ENGRAVINGS
OF THE MOST CELEBRATED
BUILDINGS IN NEWCASTLE
AND NEIGHBOURHOOD,
TO WHICH IS ADDED A GUIDE TO NEWCASTLE.

Newcastle-upon-Tyne:
PUBLISHED BY
THOMAS ALLAN, 16, COLLINGWOOD STREET,
AND 45, DEAN STREET.
NORTH SHIELDS:—RALPH ALLAN. CHURCH WAY.

Thomas Allan, A Choice Collection of Tyneside Songs, 1865.

George Stanley now lived at 45 Cumberland Place,[248] but in October a mysterious fire 'considerably charred' the Tyne Concert Hall.[249] In December, Stanley ran Darlington Theatre Royal;[250] but by 1866 'a party of capitalists' was building a new theatre in Westgate Street, Newcastle. Stanley had shares in the company, but he reopened the Tyne.[251]

Mr T. Stirling sang Ridley's 'Comic Song', *Cusby Butterfield*, at a working men's concert in Consett.[252]

Adam E. Donald's Grainger concert room in Newcastle closed,[253] but he became landlord of the Crown and Thistle, at 7 and 9 Groat Market. Early in 1867, a man who stole a ham from his larder spent six months in prison.[254] Thomas Allan lived at 14 Alexandra Terrace, Sandyford, while Ralph lived at 195 Linskill Street, North Shields, and had a newsagent's shop at 23 Tyne Street.[255]

In the summer, Stanley announced that the Tyne Concert Hall had attracted 1,316, 247 customers for 1,169 performances, at an average of 1,125 for around 200 nights a year; but he needed a 'First-class DRAMATIC COMPANY and ORCHESTRA' for the largest concert hall in the north of England. He asked applicants to write to his home address, but later delegated the 'remaining Vacancies' to a London agent. He announced that the box and pit entrances to the new theatre were in Westgate Street and the gallery and stage doors were in Thornton Street. The theatre would 'accommodate nearly Three Thousand'. The 'The Private and Dress Boxes' were in 'a *recherché* and elegant style' and held 'Four Hundred' people. The Upper Circle held 'Three Hundred and Eighty; the Spacious Pit, One Thousand; and the Extensive Gallery, Eleven Hundred'. Thomas Forster was the nominal owner, but Stanley was the sole lessee and manager, and the magistrates gave him a dramatic licence in mid-September.[256] The *Newcastle Courant* reported that Gallery seats had backs, the Dress Circle had chairs and the upholstery of the chairs in the upper boxes was crimson leather. The front of the building was sandstone and firebricks,[257] so some of the materials, and almost certainly some of the £20,000 to 30,000 of capital investment, came from the Cowens.

The Tyne Theatre and Opera House opened on 23 September in the middle of a scare about 'Fenians' – Irish revolutionary nationalists – who police claimed were drilling on Tyneside. The play was Dion Boucicault's *Arrah-na-Pogue*, about Irish rebels in the revolutionary days of 1798, and the audiences no doubt included many of Newcastle's twenty thousand Irish immigrants.[258] Stanley noted that the 'commercial panic of 1866' had 'completely paralysed Theatricals' and the last three years had been 'the worst the theatrical profession has experienced since I have known it';[259] but he praised the 'honest and intelligent artisans' who were staunch patrons.[260]

The Reform Act increased the size of the Irish vote,[261] and Joseph Cowen junior was re-elected to Newcastle council in 1868.[262]Adam E. Donald died that spring, aged 42. In autumn, John Balmbra died in Wharnecliffe Street, aged 61.[263] The Probate Calendar described him as a 'Gentleman', and noted that he had left Isabella, his widow and sole beneficiary, 'under £600'.

In 1869, Elizabeth Stephenson, George Ridley's grandmother, died in Grahamsley Street, Gateshead, aged 76. Tommy Armstrong, 'The Pitman poet', wrote *Tanfield Brake*, about 'Coffee Jack' and an accident-prone vehicle, and set it to the tune of *Blaydon Races*.[264] Mrs Forster Margaret Donald, Adam's widow, was now landlady of the Crown and Thistle in Newcastle.[265] In 1870, Thomas Stephenson, George Ridley's uncle, died aged 56. Thomas Allan married 21-year-old Annie Armstrong, the daughter of Edward Armstrong of Newcastle.[266] The Jockey Club derecognised races like Blaydon with stakes of less than one hundred guineas a day.[267]

By 1871, Matthew and Frances Ridley lived at 1 Grahamsley Street, Gateshead. David, a labourer, and Benjamin, a coal miner, lived with their parents, and they shared the house with nine others, but the rest of their siblings lived independently.

John lived in Scott's Buildings, Pipewellgate. He was a coal miner, and his 35-year-old wife, Elleanor, was a shopkeeper'. Fifteen-year-old Hannah and ten-year-old Elizabeth were at school, and Mary was one.

Matthew was 'Furrier'. He and his 32-year-old wife, Elizabeth, lodged at 84 High West Street with Robert Scott, a 'Shipping Foreman' from Wooler.

Young was a 'Wire Rope maker', and lived at 37 Carrick Street, with his 31-year-old wife, Elizabeth, from Berwick.

Elizabeth junior, aged seven, and Caroline, aged five, had been born in Newcastle, but Mary, aged three, and Young junior, aged six weeks, were born in Gateshead.

'Joseph' Stephenson Ridley, a 'Hatter', lodged at the William IV, Bensham Road, and married Janet Ann Hetherington.

Mary was a 'Domestic Servant' for butcher Henry Rowell at 281 High Street.

Ralph and Ann Allan lived at Jackson Street, North Shields, with their children Ralph, James, Isabella and Ethel. Thomas and Annie Allan lived at 14 and 15 Alexandra Place, Sandyford, Newcastle, with her 29-year-old sister Elizabeth Armstrong.[268] Thomas Allan junior arrived late that year. Reportedly, 'few men had a better knowledge of the various efforts' for 'the improvement of the people' than Thomas Allan senior and his 'knowledge of the early leaders of the Temperance Movement, and his active sympathy with them' was 'unequalled in the North of England'.[269]

Joe Wilson had become a successful singer-songwriter. In 1869, he had married Isabella English of Jarrow, and their first child was born in 1870. In 1871, the 'Tyneside Comedian' was unsuccessful at running a concert hall in Spennymoor, so he borrowed money to become a pub landlord in Bridge Street, Newcastle; but he hated dealing with drunks, so he left in 1872 and joined the Good Templars. According to Thomas Allan, the capital was 'honourably repaid'. Wilson helped Thomas Fordyce to set type for a new edition of Allan's songbook, [270] and Allan summarised Ridley's achievements.

> As a song writer it cannot be said that his songs have the literary merit of the older Tyneside writers but considering under what disadvantages he wrote, his premature death and how little fitted his life was to foster literary inclinations his

songs are exceedingly good And it must not be forgotten that they were written for his own purposes as a Concert hall singer and there they did sing And now eight Years after his death at social meetings and private parties where his songs are often sung they never fail to please [u]ndoubtedly had he not fallen as it were at the opening of his career he would have left a still more indellible mark as a Tyneside song writer.[271]

Gateshead had produced another 'local' singer-songwriter. Around 1864, 23-year-old Rowland Harrison appeared at the Victoria Music Hall and in Newcastle and in South Shields, Sunderland, Stockton, Darlington and Glasgow.[272] Probably in 1872, Thomas Allan published *Rowland Harrison's Tyneside songs no.1*.[273] The numbers appeared as a book,[274] and Allan probably owned the copyright.[275]

Probably at this time, the *Chronicle* became aware of an 'Illustrated Edition of Tyneside Songs' in 'fortnightly numbers'.

The numbers that have already appeared contain some of the popular songs of Mr. E. Corvan and Mr. George Ridley, but the succeeding parts are to contain selections from the Tyneside poets generally. The publication is neatly printed, and of a handy shape and size, and will, no doubt, secure a considerable sale.[276]

A
CHOICE COLLECTION
OF
TYNESIDE SONGS,
BY
WILSON, CORVAN, MITFORD, GILCHRIST, HARRISON, ROBSON, EMERY, RIDLEY, OLIVER, SHIELD, &c., &c.;
WITH
LIVES OF THE AUTHORS.
ILLUSTRATED WITH
VIEWS OF THE TOWN,
AND
PORTRAITS OF THE POETS & ECCENTRICS
OF NEWCASTLE.

Newcastle-upon-Tyne:
PUBLISHED BY
ALLAN, 62, DEAN STREET, AND 16, COLLINGWOOD STREET.
NORTH SHIELDS: RALPH ALLAN, TYNE STREET.
1872.

Thomas Allan, A Choice Collection of Tyneside Songs, 1872.

Allan bound the six 16-page numbers and four 48-page sections as a book, but without a page 181. He noted that the 'first half of the present volume has been before the public for some years', but 'to make it more complete, the latter half is added'. The 'task of supplying the omission' of songwriters' biographies was 'one of difficulty', because they were, 'with few exceptions, of humble life – following their lowly occupations of painters, shoemakers, printers &c.', but 'little known beyond the immediate circle of their relatives and acquaintances'. He included a brief biography of Ridley, the engraving of him as John Higgins and 15 of his songs, including *Cushey Butterfield*, but not *Teasdale Wilson*.[277] (The rower had died of 'consumption' – tuberculosis – in North Shore, Newcastle, in 1870.[278]) Ridley was eighth on the title page, but one of his younger brothers had a national reputation.

In 1854, 'J. Stephen Ridley' – formerly Stephenson – had raced 'two well-known pedestrians' around the Newcastle Town Moor racecourse in front of 6,000 spectators, for a prize of £60. He was 'quite a novice', but won by 40 yards, and offered to race one of the others twice round the course for £20 a side.[279] In 1868, 'J.S. Ridley' came fourth in a race in Sheffield.[280] In 1869, he was the starter of a race at Gateshead, in front of 500 spectators, and Joseph Hogg, one of George Ridley's heroes, was the judge.[281] In 1871, Stephen Ridley gave competitors 50 to 180 yards start in the One Mile Sensation Handicap in Gateshead, but won.[282] He also beat the Mile Champion of England for £100, a cup, [283] and a silver belt. Early in 1872, in Manchester, 'the celebrated J. Nuttall' and 'the no less well known J. Stephen Ridley of Gateshead' raced over 1,000 yards for £25 a side in front of 1,000 spectators, but Ridley lost by a yard and a half.[284] That summer, he refereed a foot race at Gateshead Borough

Gardens,[285] lost a race against J. Davidson of Jarrow,[286] and refereed a quoits match.[287] He retained his position as Mile Champion of England at Friar's Goose,[288] and had himself photographed in his skimpy running gear along with his silver belt.

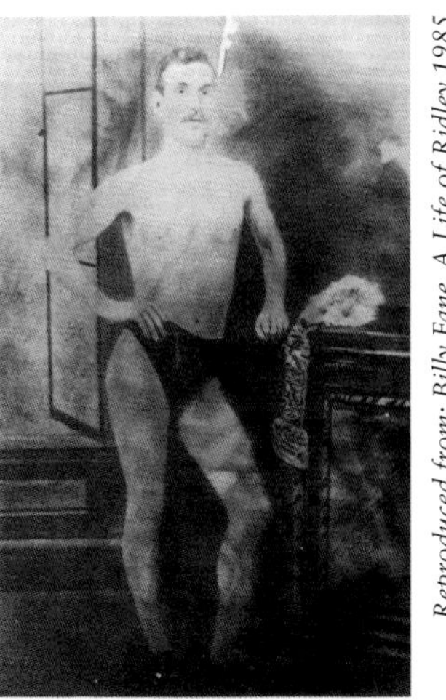

Reproduced from: Billy Fane, A Life of Ridley 1985

Stephen Ridley.

In 1873, in front of 'upwards of ten thousand supporters' at Gateshead Borough Gardens, and with 'a great deal of money on the race', he lost the Mile Challenge Cup by three yards.[289] Soon after, the North Eastern Railway built engine sheds on the track.[290]

Thomas Allan was now a 'Wholesale Bookseller' in Dean Street and Collingwood Street, Newcastle, and published Joe Wilson's *Tyneside Songs, Ballads and Drolleries*, which Ralph Allan also sold in Tyne Street, North Shields.[291] Thomas reissued *A Choice Collection of Tyneside Songs*, which sold for four shillings.[292] The first, fourth, fifth and sixth 16-page numbers were re-set, and Ridley remained eighth on the title page, but the engraving of him as Higgins and Allan's biography appeared with a Wilson acrostic.

R eady was he wi' the "Bobby Cure, "
I n Stanley's Hall, te myek secure
D elight tiv a' the patrons there,
L iked be them a', – but noo, ne mair
E nlivenin strains frae him ye'll hear,
Y e'll knaw ne mair poor Geordys cheer.

Allan included 12 Ridley songs, [293] but not *The Blaydon Keelman*, *Bullerwell and Summer's Race*, *The Rifleman* or *Teasdale Wilson*.

Joseph Cowen senior had recently received a knighthood, but he died in December 1873.[294] Joseph junior had his printed by-election propaganda ready for posting, and was elected as MP for Newcastle in January 1874, but Parliament was dissolved before he could take his seat. Cowen was re-elected, but was too ill to go to London.[295]

Thomas and George Allan had a shop at 26 Blackett Street,[296] which had belonged to James Watson, a bookseller and veteran Chartist who went to prison for selling unstamped publications.[297] Ralph Allan senior's shop was at Church Way, North Shields.[298] By spring, Joe Wilson had sold the copyright of some of his songs to Thomas Allan, who published 36-page, two-penny parts of *Temperance Songs, Readings, and Recitations, in the Tyneside Dialect, Comic and Sentimental*,[299] and later had them bound as a book.[300] Matthew Ridley, George's father, died that summer, aged 66.

In October, 'NEW BOOKS AT REDUCED PRICES ON SALE AT ALLAN'S' included 'ALLAN'S ILLUSTRATED EDITION OF TYNESIDE SONGS', the 'most complete collection of old favourite Tyneside Songs in print'. The Allans had cut the price of the 'Strongly-bound' edition from four shillings to three shillings and fourpence,[301] and Volume I of a larger edition of *A Choice Collection of Tyneside Songs* probably appeared in time for Christmas. The first, fourth, fifth and sixth 16-page numbers were re-set and there were six 14-page sections, while the undated Volume II included six 32-page sections, all of which were probably available separately. The books included 11 Ridley songs from the previous edition, but not *Bullerwell and Summer's Race*.[302] The two volumes, with an Index, cost four shillings.[303] It was to be the last edition of Allans' songbook for 17 years.

9 *Allan's illustrated edition of Tyneside Songs*

In January 1875, Joe Wilson died aged 33,[304] 'after a lingering illness', and was buried at old Jesmond Cemetery. In February, *The Era* reported that the *Newcastle Chronicle* staff would act as trustees for a subscription for his widow and three children.[305] The *Chronicle* advertised 'Mr. Fordyce's collection of Joe Wilson's songs'; but Fordyce was the printer, not the publisher, so next day the paper credited the book to 'Mr Allan'. George Stanley donated two guineas to the subscription and Thomas and George Allan three guineas;[306] but two months later one of Isabella Wilson's children died.[307] Frances Ridley, George's mother, died that summer, aged 65.

In 1876, *Johnny Luik-Up* appeared in the *Newcastle Weekly Chronicle,* without the last four lines, but with a note about John Higgins.

> A candyman, in pitman's parlance, is now any sort of waif and stray irregular, Bashi-Bazouks [Turkish for 'damaged heads'] such as flock like cormorants or vultures, to a colliery, on the commencement of a strike, to assist in evicting people from their houses. But Johnny Higgins was far above that kind of thing. His lowest flights were to wind-mills and painted bladders, the monkey up the stick, and a lucky bag. In his latter days, we are told, he had a good business as a house agent.[308]

Just before Christmas, the *Newcastle Courant* described 62 Dean Street.

> At the head of this street is the large corner shop of Messrs Allan, which has not the slightest character of taste or elegance, and, indeed, this is not what the proprietors have striven to

acquire ... As a shop for the million, as a depot of endless light literature, new and old – that scrappy lore, 'understand the common people', Mr Allan's shop has no rival in Newcastle, except its own offshoots in Blackett Street and Collingwood Street. In the publication of the local bards, Joe Wilson, Ned Corvan, G. Ridley, and others, Mr Allan has done his best to 'please, instruct, amuse', and give a wide popularity to the vernacular rhymes of canny Newcastle, so as to impress even a stranger with the 'gud opinion' of each native strain.[309]

The Wilson subscription eventually reached £1,000 ;[310] but by 1877, 'Mrs Joe Wilson' was performing at the Star Theatre of Varieties in Stockton.[311] The Allans' Blackett Street shop was at number 28.[312]

In 1878, Thomas Allan supervised the building of two large houses in Osborne Avenue, Jesmond. One was for his wife and children, and the other for his siblings George and Elizabeth, but he divided them 'mid-stream' to 'make a third between them' for William and his wife.[313] In 1879, *Johnny Luik-Up* reappeared in the *Weekly Chronicle*, but without the note on Higgins.[314]

In 1881, Ralph Allan, 'Bookseller & Stationer', lived at 3 Beaumont Street, North Shields. Ralph junior had left, but Ethel, Isabella and James lived at home, and James helped to run the shop. In Newcastle, Thomas and George Allan ran the Blackett Street and Collingwood Street shops and William ran 62 Dean Street.[315] Thomas employed eight men, three women, two boys and two girls, and lived at 91 Osborne Villas with Annie and her 40-year-old sister, Elizabeth Armstrong. Thomas junior was a 'Scholar' as were seven-year-old Edward and five-year-old George William. At number 92, William Allan, 'Bookseller' and 'Stationer', lived with his 29-year-old wife Mary Elizabeth, three-year-old William, and 25-year-old Isabella C. Strother, a 'General

Servant' originally from Coxhoe, County Durham. At number 93, George Allan, 'Bookseller & Stationer', lived with his 50-year-old wife, Elizabeth, his 39-year-old brother, Nicholas, a 'Bookseller's Assistant', and 16-year-old Elizabeth Todd, a 'General Servant' from Newburn, Northumberland.

John Ridley, George's brother, was still a coal miner, and lived at 9 Tidd's Yard, Gateshead. Hannah was his 'Housekeeper'. Mary aged 11, was a 'Scholar', as was Matthew, aged six, while 'Belle' – Isabella – was three. John's wife, 'Ellen' – Elena – was a 'Hawker', and lodged with her sister, Ann, and her brother-in-law, Robert Brown, a 'Provision Dealer', at 2 Ellison Street West, Gateshead.

Matthew Ridley was a 'Rent Collecting Clerk', and lodged at 133 Upper Albert Road, Midlesbrough, with Rees Davies, a 'Manager of Ironworks' who was born in 'Merthyr Tydvill'.

Young Ridley was a foreman at a 'Wire Ropery' in Harton, between South Shields and Sunderland, and he and Elizabeth lived at 15 Eleanor Terrace. Elizabeth junior had no outside occupation, but Caroline was a 'Pupil Teacher'. Mary was a 'Scholar', as were Young junior and Isabella, aged seven.

'Joseph S. Ridley' – Stephenson – was a labourer and lived at 33 Tent Street, Gateshead, with Janet and five-year-old Benjamin. Benjamin Ridley, Joseph's brother, was a lodger.

In 1882, George Ridley's *Bobby the Cure* appeared in the *Newcastle Weekly Chronicle*,[316] and in 1885, the *Newcastle Weekly Courant* referred to 'Geordie Ridley'.[317] Thomas Allan had been a 'Radical', and was now a wealthy Liberal, but the party split over Home Rule for Ireland. His 'leaning towards conservatism made itself felt amongst his friends', and he joined the Liberal Unionists, who soon merged with the Conservatives. His daughter Kate was born in 1886, [318] but soon died. Thomas published Joe Wilson's *Temperance*

Songs in runs of 1,000 and aimed to make 200 per cent profit. His brother Ralph had a stationer's shop at 14 Church Way, a bookbinder's at 23 Saville Street and a bookshop at 23 Tyne Street. Ralph junior was a stationer's assistant at 10 Cecil Street. By 1887, Ralph senior sold books from home and Ralph junior ran a bookshop at 10 Cecil Street.[319] His uncle, Nicholas Allan, died aged 45. George Ridley's sister, Elizabeth, died in Sunderland, aged 54. In 1888, 'Joseph Stevenson' Ridley died at 25 Tent Street, Gateshead, aged 44.

In the 1870s, the *Newcastle Daily Chronicle*'s circulation had been 35,000 , higher than any provincial daily or 'advanced Liberal' paper, and it sometimes reached 45,000 ; but its staff was ageing.

> There was one man who had taken part in the liberation of Italy ... [and] it would have been possible to meet a quiet, white-haired, dignified gentleman who had carried over from London to Paris the pistols which played their part in one of the attempted assassinations on Napoleon III. Another member of the staff had edited a Republican journal [and] a fourth had played an active part in securing the escape of more than one patriot from the prisons of European despotism.[320]

Joseph Cowen attended the Commons for the first time in 1876, but he saw being a Liberal MP as a 'perfectly useless occupation' by 1878,[321] and called himself a 'Radical' by 1879.[322] He was re-elected in 1880, but left the Newcastle Liberal Association and took a third of the members with him. In 1881, he corresponded with Karl Marx, and Friedrich Engels described Cowen as 'half, if not a whole communist'. Cowen joined the Democratic Federation, but left after it became the Social Democratic Federation, and associated with the Russian Prince Peter Kropotkin and émigré anarchists. In 1885, Cowen narrowly topped the poll in the parliamentary election, thanks to Tory votes,[323] and was now an outspoken nationalist and imperialist.[324] He did not stand in 1886, but he bailed out the SDF's Henry Hyndman, after his arrest at the London riots.[325] In 1889, there were 20,000 spectators at Blaydon races near Stella Hall.[326]

By 1890, Ralph Allan senior had retired, but Ralph junior had shops at 14 Church Way and 29A Saville Street, North Shields.[327]

The Allans erected a stone on Joe Wilson's grave and the *Chronicle* reported that it cost £38. A photograph appeared in the Allans' 'Collected Edition' of Joe Wilson's *Tyneside Songs and Drolleries, Readings and Temperance Songs*, which was dedicated to Cowen. 'A VOLUME which, in the dialect of Tyneside, depicts the everyday life of the people, may, it is thought, be fittingly inscribed to one who, always partial to what is "racy of the soil, " has, from his earliest days, toiled for the elevation of the masses'.[328] The Allans expected a profit of 29 per cent and Cowen's *Chronicle* gave away a free lithograph of Wilson.[329]

George Benson published *Blaydon Races* as a slip song (see page 110), in time for the Whit races, but had to acknowledge the 'kind permission' of the copyright owners, 'Messrs. T. and G. Allan'.

By 1891, John Ridley had died. 'Ellen', his widow, was still a hawker, and lived in part of 13 Mulgrave Terrace, Gateshead, with her daughters, Mary, a 'Domestic Servant', and Isabella, a 'Scholar'.

Matthew Ridley lived in Harton, County Durham with his wife, 49-year-old 'Joann', born in Helson Bell, Northumberland.

Young Ridley, a 'Wire Rope Maker, lived at 1 Wilkinson Terrace, Harton, with Elizabeth. Mary was an 'Ex pupil teacher', while Young junior and 17-year-old Isabella were in full-time education.

BLAYDON RACES,

WHIT-MONDAY, MAY 26TH, 1890.

[*Copyright by kind permission of Messrs. T. and G. Allan, Stationers, Dean Street and Blackett Street, Newcastle-upon-Tyne.*]

Aw went to Blaydon Races, 'twas on the ninth of Joon,
Eiteen hundred an' sixty two, on a summer's efternoon,
Aw tuck the 'bus frae Balmbra's an' she wis heavy laden,
Away we went alang Collingwood Street, that's on the road to Blaydon.

CHORUS.

O lads, ye shud only seen us gannin,
We passed the foaks upon the road just as they wor stannin;
Thor wes lots o' lads an' lasses there, all wi' smiling faces,
Gan alang the Scotswood Road, to see the Blaydon Races.

We flew past Airmstrang's factory, and up to the "Robin Adair,"
Just gannin doon te the railway bridge, the 'bus wheel flew off there.
The lasses lost their crinolines off, an' the veils that hide their faces,
An' aw got two black eyes an' a broken nose in gan to Blaydon Races.
Chorus—O lads, &c.

When we gat the wheel put on away we went agyen,
But them that had their noses broke, they cam' back ower hyem,
Sum went to the Dispensary, an' uthers to Doctor Gibb's,
An' sum sought out the Infirmary to mend their broken ribs.
Chorus—O lads, &c.

Noo when we gat to Paradise thor wes bonny gam begun,
Thor wes fower-and-twenty on the 'bus, man, hoo they danced an' sung;
They called on me to sing a sang, aw sung them "Paddy Fagan,"
Aw danced a jig an' swung my twig that day aw went to Blaydon.
Chorus—O lads, &c.

We flew across the Chain Bridge reet into Blaydon toon,
The bellman he was callin there—they call him Jackey Brown,
Aw saw him talkin to sum cheps, an' them he was pursuadin'
To gan an' see Geordy Ridley's concert in the Mechanics' Hall at Blaydon.
Chorus—O lads, &c.

The rain it poor'd aw the day, an' myed the groon'd quite muddy,
Coffy Johnny had a white hat on—they war shootin' "Whe stole the cuddy."
There wes spice stalls an' munkey shows, an' aud wives selling ciders,
An' a chep wiv a happeny roond aboot shootin' now, me boys, for riders.
Chorus—O lads, &c.

Printed for George Benson at the "Daily Journal" Office, Clayton Street, Newcastle.

Blaydon Races (Allan Papers).

Benjamin Ridley, a 'General Labourer', lived at 2 Grahamsley Street, Gateshead, with his wife, Jane, and their three children. Thomas was a 'General Labourer', John was fourteen and Frances was two.

Ralph Allan, 'Bookseller', his wife Ann, and one daughter had 3 Beaumont Street, North Shields, to themselves, since the other three children had evidently left home.

Thomas and Annie Allan's three teenage boys had all worked for the family's shops since they left school, [330] and lived with their parents at 9 Osborne Villas, Jesmond, Newcastle. Thomas Allan was a 'Bookseller, Stat[ioner] and Newsagent', and Annie's sister, Elizabeth Armstrong, was a 'Boarder', but 'Living on own means'. Thomas junior was a 'Bookseller's assistant', as were Edward and George. Nine-year-old Flora Alice was a 'Scholar', as was six-year-old Annie junior, while Elizabeth was two. Eighteen-year-old Mary Ann Pickford, a 'General Servant (domestic)', was from Parkins Vale, County Durham.

At number 11 Osborne Villas, George Allan, a 'Bookseller' and 'stationer', lived with sister Elizabeth, and Hannah Gibbons, a 'General Servant', born in Sunnybrow, near Bishop Auckland.

Number 10 Osborne Villas was evidently vacant. William Allan now lived at 1 North Terrace, Newcastle, with Mary, William junior, Alice, aged nine, and Nora J., aged five, plus 11 Thomas L. Hedley, William's nephew. Twenty-nine-year-old Catherine Richardson, a 'general domestic serv[ant]', hailed from Winlaton.

Late in 1891, the Allans published a large songbook.

The smaller edition cost four shillings, but the larger, 'De Luxe', edition cost seven shillings.[331] The Allans dedicated the 594-page book to the antiquarian, Richard Oliver Heslop. It included George Ridley's *Joey Jones*, *Blaydon Races*,

ALLAN'S

ILLUSTRATED EDITION

OF

TYNESIDE SONGS

AND READINGS.

WITH

LIVES, PORTRAITS, AND AUTOGRAPHS OF THE WRITERS,

AND NOTES ON THE SONGS.

REVISED EDITION.

NEWCASTLE-UPON-TYNE:
THOMAS & GEORGE ALLAN,
18 BLACKETT STREET, AND 34 COLLINGWOOD STREET.
SOLD BY
W. ALLAN, 30 GRAINGER STREET; R. ALLAN, NORTH SHIELDS.
LONDON: WALTER SCOTT.
1891

Left, Allan's Illustrated Edition of Tyneside Songs, 1891.

Right, George Ridley as Higgins (Allan Papers).

Chambers, *The Sheels Lass for Me*, *The Bobby Cure*, *Johnny Luik-Up!*, *John Spencer* and *The Stephenson Monument*, from the 'Author's Manuscript 1862', a longer biography and the engraving of him as Higgins,[332] but it had been cropped to show only the ragged child's finger-ends.

One local newspaper review mentioned Ridley in passing, but others ignored him completely.[333]

In 1892, the *Newcastle Courant* noted that Blaydon races were 'somewhat reproachfully spoken of, probably owing to the rough, homespun verses, by which a Tyneside Bard has "immortalised" it'.[334]

On New Year's Day 1893, Thomas Allan began composing 'an autobiographical sketch'. 'It was not that I had anything in particular to relate. I should think that few who have reached their 60th year have had less but the reciting will amuse myself and interest my family, and possibly a few beyond that limited circle'. By spring, he had a stomach tumour.[335] Young Ridley senior died in South Shields, aged around 53.

Thomas Allan (Allan Papers).

Thomas Allan died on 8 April 1894, aged 61, and was buried in St Andrew's Cemetery on 11 April.[336]

His sons Thomas, Edward and George William took over his shops.[337] Their uncle Ralph still lived at 3 Beaumont Place, North Shields, and their cousin Ralph at 23 Grosvenor Place.[338]

In Newcastle, Peter Nelson had become landlord of the Wheat Sheaf in 1893.

Vin Arthey

The Wheat Sheaf.

Nelson owed £567, but agreed to pay £200 a year in rent, plus £4 a week for the 'fixtures'. Later, he agreed to pay £1,000 for the 'fixtures' and handed over £500; but his expenses were never less than £20 a week and his only income came from the sale of drink, so he 'lost heavily' and was bankrupt by 1895.[339] That year, David Ridley, George's brother, died in Gateshead, aged 45.

In the 1870s, the Tyne Theatre and Opera House had not been financially successful and George Stanley had 'surrendered' the lease to Mr R.W. Younge in 1881. Stanley had some success as an actor and producer in the USA, but returned to live in London, where he had acting engagements, wrote for theatrical periodicals and 'supplied dramas and pantomimes to various theatres'. He died in 1898 aged 75.[340] George Allan senior also died that year.[341] After a fire in 1899, the Wheat Sheaf was completely demolished.[342]

William Irving was born into a farming family in Ainsdale, Cumberland, in 1866. He later studied at the Newcastle School of Art and became an illustrator for Cowen's *Newcastle Weekly Chronicle*; but it was using photographs by 1895, so Irving painted portraits and landscapes, and he exhibited at the Royal Academy in 1898.[343]

In 1900, Blaydon races had over 10,000 spectators.[344] Joseph Cowen died,[345] and Irving painted a posthumous portrait of him.[346]

'Coffee Johnny' – John Wilson – died in his early seventies.[347] 'Jackey Broon', the Blaydon Bellman, died in 1901, aged 82,[348] but the Wheat Sheaf had been rebuilt.[349]

Coffee Johnny.

Ralph Allan senior, 'Stationer', was living at 7 Alma Place, Tynemouth with his wife Ann and their daughters, Isabella, a 'Stationers' Clerk', and Ethel. Ralph's brother, William, died that year, aged 57.[350]

Matthew Ridley, a labourer, lived at 149 Barrass Bridge, Newcastle, with his wife Joan and a 57-year old servant, 'Wilkelmind', from Scotland.

Benjamin Ridley, a 'Black Smith Striker', and his wife Jane, lived at 33 Chanders Street, Gateshead, with 14-year-old John, a 'mineral water worker', nine-year-old Frances, seven-year-old Thomas, four-year-old Benjamin, and James Jordinson, a 50-year-old 'Hirbalist Submed', born in Hull.

Irving began painting *Blaydon Races – A Study from Life* at home in Ovingham. Its 26 Tyneside 'characters' included 'Coffee Johnny' with his white hat and 'Cushie Butterfield' below him on the right.[351]

William Irving, Blaydon Races. (TWAM)

In 1903, James Deuchar, the owner of Monkwearmouth Brewery, bought Irving's painting. It appeared in Mawson, Swan and Morgan's art gallery window in Grainger Street, Newcastle, and 'attracted such large crowds that passing traffic was brought to a standstill', so 'the police asked the manager to draw the blinds'. Deuchar later installed the painting in the County Hotel in Neville Street, Newcastle.[352]

Around 1906, the lyrics of *Blaydon Races* appeared on posters advertising the races, [353] but then the event lapsed for a decade.[354]

Ralph Allan senior died in 1909.[355] Ralph junior 'went into cinemas', and Thomas's sons, Edward and George William, took over Ralph's stationery business.[356]

In 1911, Annie Allan, Thomas's widow, lived at 9 Osborne Villas, Jesmond, on 'Private Means', with her sister, Elizabeth Armstrong, and four unmarried children. Edward was a 'Bookseller, Stationer (Dealer)', as was George William. Flora Alice and Elizabeth were still at home. Annie Oxwell, a 22-year-old 'General Servant', was from Swalwell.

Matthew Ridley was 74, and Joanne, was 69. Benjamin Ridley, a 'Labourer', and Jane lived with their sons John, a 'Labourer', Thomas, a 'Coal Putter' and Benjamin junior, who was at school. All five inhabited just one room at 8 Grahamsley Street, Gateshead. Frances had left home or died.

Elizabeth, Young senior's widow, lived at 199 West Park View, South Shields, with Mary, Young junior and Isabella, who were all schoolteachers.

Janet Ann Ridley, Joseph Stephenson's widow, shared three rooms at 27 Tent Street with her sons Joseph, a 'Warehouseman', Richard, a 'Goods Porter, and her six-year-old niece, Elizabeth Jane, who was at school. Mary Elizabeth Waitt was a 'General Servant Domestic'. William Eccleston, a 37-year-old 'Mason's Labourer, and 20-year-old Francis

Robinson, a 'General Carter', were boarders.

Janet Ann's daughters, Frances, born in 1877, and Margaret, born in 1884, had left home or died. Janet Ann's son, Robert, a 'Railway Bridge Painter', lived with his 40-year-old wife, Esther. Their daughter, Susannah, a 'Mineral water Bottler', was 19, Joseph Stephenson junior, an 'Engine Cleaner', was 17. Robert, Thomas Cooper, aged ten, and Esther junior, aged eight, were at school. John George was four, Margaret Jane was two and Janet Ann junior was one month. All ten squashed into two rooms at 31 Briscoe Street, Gateshead. Janet Ann's son, George, a 'Bridge Painter', was married to Sarah, who was 26, and lived at 18 North Street, Gateshead. Janet Ann's son, John, a 'Goods Porter', and his 22-year-old wife, Elizabeth Ann, lived at 24 Berwick Street, Gateshead.

John Ridley's son, Matthew, an 'Engine Painter', and his wife, Margaret, lived at 16 Easton Court, Gateshead. Sarah Jane was seven, John was five, Margaret junior was two and Elizabeth was eight months. Hannah Ridley, John senior's sister, lived with them. Their sisters, Elizabeth and Mary, have not been traced; but two of their late uncle George's songs were about to take on a new lease of life.

10 Catchy

Robert Catcheside was born in Newcastle in 1815. By 1841, he and his brother George were grocers and tea-dealers in St Nicholas's Square, Newcastle. Robert, who lived in St James Street, Benwell, [357] married Mary Dodds. Robert Marium was born in 1842, but Mary died in 1846, aged about 30.[358] In 1848, Robert senior signed a petition to the government against increased military expenditure.[359] By 1850, he and George were living at Ridley Villas, Newcastle.[360] In 1851, Robert signed a petition for the repeal of stamp duty on newspapers and married Louisa Mary Gowdy, the daughter of a deceased Royal Navy Captain, in Liverpool. Robert was 36,[361] and she was 19.[362] In 1854, he supported the fund for the widows and orphans of soldiers killed in the Crimea; and he became a poor law auditor and assessor for St Andrew's South Ward in 1858.

Charles Ernest Catcheside was born in 1860. By 1861, the family lived at 20 East Parade, Elswick. Robert and Mary had four sons, aged between eight and one, plus a 'General Servant' and a 'Nurse'. By 1871, Charles was a 'Scholar', and had a sister, and the family had two servants. In 1881, the children, including a second girl, lived with their parents. Charles was 'Clerk to Borough Treasurer'. In 1882, 'Mr. C. Catcheside' sang at a concert in aid of the National School in Wallsend and in 1883, he was a judge at the Horse Procession in Newcastle. He married Glasgow-born Annie Wardlaw K. McGibbon, the 24-year-old daughter of James McGibbon Esquire, in St Andrew's Church. Charles was a presiding officer at the election of a councillor in All Saints West Ward. In 1884, he took part in a dramatic and musical entertainment at the Aquarium in Tynemouth, in aid of the Northumberland Village Homes, and he was the accompanist and conductor at a concert after the annual inspection of Newcastle Corporation's horses. Mona was born that year, and Bertha followed in 1885. Robert senior died aged 69, but 'Chas Catcheside' joined the committee of the Gosforth Amateur Vocal Society. In 1887, 'Mrs C. Catcheside' sang at a Stannington concert.[363]

In 1867, Charles' brother Robert had married Sophia Bennehan, the 22-year-old daughter of an Irish piano-maker, in Manchester; but she died of tuberculosis in 1870.[364] By 1872, Robert sang professionally as 'Ernest Sheldon',[365] and in 1887 he married Ada Livermore, the sister of Horace and Lechmere, 'Proprietors of the only Court Minstrels'.[366] In 1889, Charles sang in an opera at Kilburn Town Hall in London, as 'Ernest Warrington'.[367] 'Sheldon', a tenor, sang with the Court Minstrels,[368] and Charles, a baritone, became their 'corner-man', carrying on humorous dialogues with all the others.[369]

Dave Gillings had blacked up as a 'minstrel' since around 1875, and later became the Court Minstrels' comic, violinist and musical director. In 1890, he and 'Charles Warrington' had their first engagement at Ephison's Circus in Hanley, Stoke-on-Trent.[370] In 1891, 'Ernest Warrington', a 'Music hall Manager', his wife, Annie, and one daughter, Mona, were boarders at the home of Francis Martin, a 'Tobacconist', at 64 Union Street, Plymouth, and Alfred Sydney, 'Theatrical Manager', was a visitor. 'Ernest Warrington' performed at St James's Hall, and was Acting Manager for the Livermore Brothers;[371] but he and Gillings also performed at the Queens Music Hall in Poplar, London.[372]

'Ernest Sheldon', 'the Variety Pioneer', managed the Livermores' 'headquarters' at the People's Palace in

Newcastle, and Charles moved there, pending the construction of the People's Palace in Bristol, which he hoped to manage.[373] Early in 1892, amid 'much interest', [374] 'Ernest Warrington' applied for a dramatic licence for the People's Palace in Sunderland,[375] and invited the Board of Guardians to see the show.[376] In spring, he described himself in *The Era* as an 'Operatic Vocalist, Pianist, Conductor, and Acting-Manager', but gave the address of his Newcastle solicitor and threatened to sue anyone who referred to him in 'a manner calculated to do me injury'. At his benefit night at the People's Palace, 'under the patronage of several Masonic lodges', the 'huge building was packed to the ceiling';[377] and Gillings and 'Warrington' also performed at the Aquarium, Palace and Collins music halls in London.[378]

In January 1893, *The Era* noted that Gillings had been 'joined by Mr. Ernest Warrington' to form 'The Mozarts', who were 'booked twelve months ahead', beginning in Plymouth, and going on to Bristol, Swansea and four London halls. In summer, Sunderland People's Palace was available to let. The Mozarts appointed Mr G.H. McDermott of London as their 'Sole Representative', and '"The Mozart's" Company' went on to play in Yarmouth, Leeds, Cambridge, Derby, Birmingham, Liverpool, Dundee and London.[379]

Jonathan Lewis Young's Edison Phonographic Office in Fore Street, London, [380] was the first sound-recording studio in Europe. Charles Catcheside recalled that the 'difficulty' was 'to get a clear and incisive voice – "a good cutter" – as their machine would not give a good result from any other'; but a friend told him that his voice was 'suitable for recording', so he had a trial and was 'engaged at once'.

Sheet music cost four shillings, or about a 'quarter of a week's wage for most working men', but top class recordings cost a week's pay.

The cylinders were soft wax and only lasted a fortnight or so, and as we made only one at a time, you may be sure I was kept very busy This was remedied later by coupling a number of machines by rubber tube to a central bunch-piece, attached to which was an ordinary speaking tube with a circular mouth-piece. I used to hire the popular songs of the day from a music seller at a penny a time and often had to read at sight, which being a musician, I was fortunately able to do … I recollect a customer coming into the office one day and asking for 'Dada's Baby Boy' which had that day been published, and while he waited, a copy was brought, wet from the press, run over on the piano by old Dobrowski … and recorded straight away, and was in a few minutes being [displayed] in a shop in Fleet Street where a machine was on view as a novelty.

A metal tube was fixed by a rubber connection to the reproducer and a dozen or more ear-pieces were attached, by which the record could be heard for the 'Small sum of one penny', as the doorman used to announce. As so few records could be made at one time, and the demand being brisk, it was no uncommon thing for me to sing 'After the Ball' or 'My Old Dutch' twenty or thirty times running, and as I heard the 'pros' singing their songs every night in the course of my own business, I was able to give a fair rendition. The not always truthful door-man called out 'Step inside and hear "My Old Dutch" as sung by Albert Chevalier' …

Catcheside was also a salesman.

I was about to take a provincial tour for a few weeks. Mr. Young asked me to fill up stock as fully as possible before leaving. For a week or two I worked very hard all day and as I was in pantomime at the Pavilion Theatre [in Liverpool] … the 'all day' and 'all night' work rather took it out of me. Yet I had been in Liverpool for only a few days when a telegramme arrived requiring my immediate return to make more titles as stock was running low …

His schedule was tight.

> [P]erform in Liverpool; supper at sleeping car train from Lime Street at 12; arrive at Euston 4.40 am; sleep in siding till 8; down to a city hotel, bath and breakfast; office at 9.30, where the staff are waiting to work with me against time. Averaging out the length of the cylinder I sang a song every 6 minutes – 2 minutes record, 4 minutes breathing time – and by half past one I had thus sung 40 times. Then took a cab back to Euston; lunch on the train, where my seat was already booked, tea at 6 o'clock; landed at Lime Street at 6.30, straight to the theatre and fulfilled my engagement …

In four days, he travelled 1,600 miles, performed four times in Liverpool and sang 160 times in London.[381]

In 1894, The Musical Mozarts based themselves in London, but had engagements in Cardiff, Leicester, Brighton, Margate, Aberdeen,[382] and Dundee,[383] before a long run in London. One Monday evening in October they

> … left their home in Brixton at 6.15; and though run into by a van in London-road, and delayed some minutes, they arrived for their first turn at Sadler's Wells at 6.50; following on to Leach's, 7.30; Star (Bermondsey), 8.30; Varieties, 9.30; Belmont's, 10.15, and doing their sixth turn at the Palace theatre at 11.00.

Another day, they did a matinée at the Palace 'as a sort of livener to their evening's work', played the Cambridge in Commercial Street and then performed again at the Palace.

In 1895, The Mozarts mainly worked in London, but had engagements in Chatham and Portsmouth. 'Catcheside, E.' sang at a testimonial benefit for 'Ernest Sheldon' in Newcastle and the Mozarts had engagements at six London halls, before going to Blackpool, Glasgow, Newcastle, South

Shields, Sunderland and Liverpool. They sailed to Johannesburg, returned, and performed in Bath and two London halls. Early in 1896, they fulfilled a long engagement in London, and then went to Bolton, Bradford, Liverpool and Portsmouth. They returned to London, but went solo after May.[384]

In 1900, German-made flat disc recordings, costing two shillings, 'began to flood the market', and in 1901 Thomas Edison invented a way of mass-producing wax cylinders. 'Charles E. Warrington', a wine agent, Annie, Mona and Bertha lived with Annie's father, James McGibbon, a wine and spirit agent, and his wife, Jessie, at 22 Delaval Road, Cullercoats. Early in 1903, Annie died.

In 1904, 'Catcheside-Warrington' recorded on shellac discs for the Edison Bell Consolidated Phonograph Company in London, and so did 'Eric Foster',[385] an imaginary singer who paid no income tax, but sounded remarkably like 'Catcheside-Warrington'.[386] In 1908, 48-year-old 'Catcheside-Warrington', giving his age as 43, married Helen Edith Harris, aged 33, in Wandsworth, London. He may have recorded a 'Tyneside Song', but another Tynesider probably started first.

James Cosgrove was born in Newcastle 1877, but it is unclear if this was the James Cosgrove in Elswick Workhouse in 1881. By 1892, Cosgrove had an engagement at the Palace Theatre, Newcastle, as 'J.C. Scatter', a 'comedian and Hungarian dancer'.[387] Most of his engagements were probably at small venues, but he married 20-year-old Isabella in 1898. In 1900, *The Era* noted that he was at the Gaiety Theatre in Hartlepool,[388] and *The Shields Daily Gazette* described him as 'a comedian and dancer of some ability' in 1901.[389] Around 1908, when double-sided discs cost four shillings, [390] 'Scatter' recorded *Blaydon Races*,[391] and he did so again in 1909.[392] In 1910, Newcastle United won the Football Association Cup. By 1911, the 'Travelling Comedian' and Isabella had six children, aged one to 13, and lived with the 'Charwoman', Kate Crony, in three rooms at 54 Mansfield Street, Newcastle.

Charles Catcheside had returned to live on Tyneside. Reportedly, he become a commercial traveller in theatrical goods,[393] yet in 1911, 'Charles Ernest Catcheside-Warrington', a 'Commercial Traveller (Wines and Spirits)', claimed to be 49 when he was two years older. He lived at 8 Windsor Terrace, South Gosforth, Newcastle, with his wife, Helen Edythe Warrington – without the 'Catcheside' – and one daughter, Mona Winifred Valerie Warrington, a 'Teacher in a private School'.

That November, 'Ernest Warrington' recorded *Cushie Butterfield*, with its final verse, for the Gramophone Company in Hayes, Middlesex,[394] and he knew an ambitious Newcastle music publisher.

James Gale Windows was born in Cowley, Oxford, in 1870, the youngest of the four sons of Joseph, a 'Police Sergeant', and his wife Jane. By 1881, Joseph was an 'Inspector of Police' and lived at 17 Princes Street, Cowley, with his second wife, Fanny, his first wife's mother, Ann Gale, and his children. James was a 'Scholar', but by 1891 he was a 'Music Seller's Assistant', and boarded with Annie Turnbull, at 158 Monday Street, Elswick, Newcastle. In 1896, he married Maud, who was also born in Oxford. By 1901, James worked as a 'Piano Dealer's Assistant', and they lived at 57 King John Street, Heaton, Newcastle, with three-year-old Maurice. By 1911, James, a 'Music & Musical Instrument Dealer' employed staff, and lived at 69 Cardigan Terrace, Heaton, with Maud, Maurice, a 'Scholar', and five-year-old Hedley. Maggie Calder, a 'General Servant Domestic'

Brian and Helen Mawson

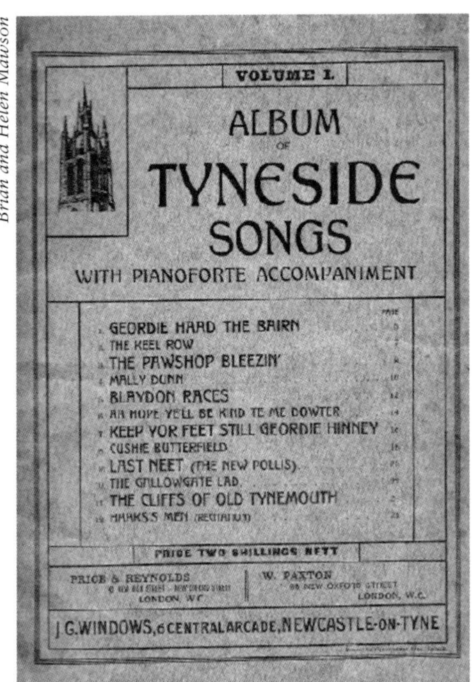

Tyneside Songs, Volume I, 1911.

from Jarrow, looked after four people and a six-room house.

Late that year, J.G. Windows of the 'Music and Pianoforte Saloons', 6, Central Arcade, Newcastle, published an *Album of Tyneside Songs*, Volume I, with 'The Tunes Collected, and the Pianoforte Part Arranged, by C.E. Catcheside-Warrington'. The 'PIANO DEALER' AND 'MUSIC SELLER' was printed by the Oppenheimer Brothers in Leipzig, and advertised 'ALL THE LATEST LONDON AND CONTINENTAL SUCCESSES', but no recordings of 'Tyneside Songs'. Some North East pitmen had pianos, but the fixed price of 'Two Shillings Nett' was a quarter of the best-paid British hewer's daily wage. 'C.E.C.-W.' wrote a Preface.

> Every district has its 'Folk Songs', and we on Tyneside are certainly blessed with a large and varied selection. But, while the words have been carefully preserved – notably in the excellent volumes published by Messrs. Allan, 20, Blackett Street, Newcastle (by whose kind permission I am allowed to use the words of several of the most popular songs) and frequently by means of the 'Weekly Chronicle' rescuing from

> oblivion the songs of our local poets, the tunes are in danger of becoming forgotten and extinct. As one who was associated with the late Dr. Bruce and Mr. John Stokoe in presenting the 'Northumberland' tunes to the public, it became an interesting hobby to collect the 'Newcassel' tunes proper, and after hoping for some years that someone more conversant with them would have printed them in a cheap and convenient form, I am now induced by many friends to present them in these pages, as much for our friends and relatives abroad as for those at home. Those who have travelled can appreciate the longing of our dear ones 'far across the sea', in whose hearts the music of Tyneside inspires all the deep, warm feeling of devotion to the 'Canny Toon' and the land of their birth; for, go where you may, the Tynesider gives way to none in the loyalty and pride one may justly feel for the home of one's youth.

He thanked Richard Oliver Heslop, 'the great authority on matters "Tyneside, "' for 'kind approval and encouragement', the editor of the *Weekly Chronicle* and 'Messrs Allan' for a second time. If Volume I met with 'the acceptance of the public', as he had been 'led to hope', there would be 'further volumes – with music – traditional and otherwise'. He dated his Preface on 'December 1911',[395] and he later confirmed this as the year of publication,[396] yet Joe Wilson's *Geordie Haad the Bairn* was 'Copyright 1912 by J.G. Windows'. 'Arranged by C.E. Warrington' appeared above every tune, but he credited no lyricists and mediated some lyrics, including *Blaydon Races*, while *Cushie Butterfield* lacked the final verse about her second lover.[397]

Windows published *Tyneside Songs* Volume II in 1912.[398] Blaydon races resumed,[399] and *Tyneside Songs* Volume III appeared in 1913.[400]

Elizabeth Armstrong, Thomas Allan's sister-in-law, died 'at the beginning of the first world war'.[401] In 1914, mass produced wax cylinders cost one shilling.[402] Reportedly *Blaydon Races,* and 'particularly the chorus', was 'a local "Tipperary" song' among 'Geordies' in the armed forces.[403] Early in 1916, George Ridley's brother, Benjamin, died aged 62. Shenanigans over betting at Blaydon races resulted in a 'riot' and the event died out.[404] Late that year, their brother John Ridley died aged 77.

Shellac was a strategically important material and German pressings factories focussed on war production. The British recording industry almost disappeared, and there were no 'Tyneside songs'.[405]

Annie Allan, Thomas's widow, died on 2 February 1924, aged 73. She left £5, 990 to her sons, Edward and George William. In March, 'Mr Catcheside Warrington (entertainer)' sang Joe Wilson's *Keep Your Feet Still, Geordy Hinney* and recited *Haak's Men* in a ten minute slot on BBC radio in Newcastle.[406] J.G. Windows Limited at the 'Piano & Music Warehouse, Central Arcade, Newcastle-on-Tyne, published *Tyneside Songs* Volume IV. It cost two shillings and sixpence, 'Nett Cash', and W. Paxton & Co. Ltd., 36-38 Dean Street, Soho, London, sold it. The 'pianoforte arrangements' were by Samuel Reay, Mus. Bac.', but the editor was 'C.E. Catcheside-Warrington' of South Gosforth. He credited no lyricists, but included two Bobby Nunn songs and one by Joe Wilson. Windows advertised dozens of 'classical' performers and orchestras on His Master's Voice recordings, and the contents of all four volumes of *Tyneside Songs*, without crediting any lyricists, but named every author included in the six volumes of their *Tyneside Stories and Recitations*, including eleven by 'C.E.C.-Warrington'.[407] That year, Newcastle United won the FA Cup.

In 1927, J.G. Windows published a 'Copyright' 'NEW EDITION' of *Tyneside Songs* Volume I. 'C.E. Catcheside-

Warrington' included a second Preface, dated from Fife Lodge, Gosforth, on 14 March, in which he claimed that he arranged the tunes in all four volumes.

> In presenting a new and revised Edition of Volume I of 'Tyneside Songs' I wish to return my thanks to the host of admirers of Tyneside and Northumbrian Folk-lore, for the great appreciation which has rewarded my efforts of the past sixteen years in collecting and editing the words and arranging the tunes of this, and the three volumes which succeeded its first appearance in 1911. The great popularity of the songs to-day, in community signing, as dance music, and as concert items, is a satisfactory evidence of the result of my labours.
>
> In response to numerous requests, I will shortly publish two more volumes of Tyneside Songs together with another volume of purely Northumbrian Songs, to all of which, I trust, Northumbrians and Tynesiders, at home and abroad, will award the same hearty support and appreciation.

These three new volumes did not appear, but J.G. Windows' target audience is clear from a sketch of well-nourished and well-dressed

Author's collection

Tyneside Songs, Volume I, 1927.

children in a large drawing room, with one girl playing a grand piano.

Windows also advertised their piano-tuning service – 'Is Your Piano well cared for?' A 'Vocabulary of Local Dialect', with advice on how to spell it, appeared 'By kind permission of the "Newcastle Weekly Chronicle"'. The editor acknowledged songwriters' names, but *Cushie Butterfield* still lacked its last verse. J.G. Windows copyrighted the 'Revised Version' of *The Keel Row*'s tune as '1912', but labelled the lyrics 'Traditional'. The price was two shillings and sixpence, 'Nett Cash'. The 'Accredited Dealers for "His Master's Voice" Radio & Records' advertised 'Records for the Lover of Serious Music', but none of 'Tyneside Songs'.[408] That summer, 'Catcheside Warrington' broadcast on BBC radio.[409] Late that year, George Ridley's last surviving brother, Matthew, died in South Shields, aged 90.

In 1928, Jamieson Dodds recorded *Cushie Butterfield* and *Blaydon Races* and 'Catcheside-Warrington' received a royalty of one penny per side. In 1929, St Hilda's Colliery Band recorded a medley that included *Blaydon Races*, and the Oxford Galleries Dance Band from Newcastle recorded the song, [410] with lyrics sung by 'Catcheside-Warrington'.[411] Dewey Gibson and 'J.C. Scatter' also recorded *Blaydon Races*, using the arrangement by 'Catcheside-Warrington'.[412] He recorded *Cushie Butterfield*, [413] and *Blaydon Races*, [414] and plugged *Tyneside Songs*.[415] Volumes II, III and IV were in their third edition.[416]

In 1931, 'Catcheside Warrington' recorded *Blaydon Races* and *Cushie Butterfield* for Edison Bell Limited in London, [418] and in 1932, Newcastle United won the Cup. In 1933, James Gale Windows died at 48 Oaklands, Gosforth, and left £8,000 to his widow, Maud, and Percival Frederick Barras, an accountant.

Probably in the mid-1930s, Jimmy Muir worked with 'Catcheside-Warrington' in Newcastle.

> I was at a special dinner in the Station Hotel when local Roman Catholic clergy entertained the Lord Bishop of Hexham and Newcastle, and on the bill were a male quartette, Catchy and myself ... six freemasons entertaining the catholics. After the show the dinner organiser inadvertently handed the fee money to Harold Woodmass instead of to Catchy. In a quiet corner, Harold counted it and made a mental note, before handing it over to Catchy, who distributed it. Half of the amount, it turned out, was for himself and the rest for the other five – just 'washers'! There was an unholy row and Woodmass called Catchy a 'bloody little villain'. As a result, I later received a five shillings postal order – additional fee – but it was the end of any further alliance with Catchy.[419]

The houses in Grahamsley Street were in poor repair. In the early 1930s, Gateshead Council acquired many

Gateshead Libraries

The rear of Grahamsley Street, Gateshead, in the 1930s.

streets in central Gateshead by compulsory purchase and demolished them,[417] but some in Grahamsley Street survived.

Gateshead Libraries

The rear of the Ridleys' former house in Grahamsley Street, 1930s.

In 1936, when a British miners' delegation visited Moscow, a band played *Blaydon Races*.[420]

Charles Edward Catcheside-Warrington died on 31 July 1937 at Fife Lodge, Stoneyhurst Road, South Gosforth, leaving £96. Jamieson Dodds recorded *Blaydon Races* and *Cushie Butterfield*.

'Scatter''s record label, Imperial, had closed in 1934,[421] but he carried on performing, and was at the Newcastle Empire in 1938. He died in Wortley Street, Newcastle, in 1943, aged 68.[422] The painter William Irving also died that year, aged 77.[423]

Once again, *Blaydon Races*, and 'particularly the chorus', was a ' rallying cry for Geordies' in the armed forces in World War II.[424] A letter-writer to *The Times* later recalled that the 'rendering' of the song by a 'Geordie' soldier at a 'company smoker' in India 'always brought down the house (we were a North Country regiment)'; while another remembered that 'the *Geordie* would sing the praises not only of the Scotswood Road but of the Cheviots'.[425]

11 'The Geordie National Anthem'

In 1947, George Ridley lay in an unmarked grave in Gateshead East Cemetery and his former home was one of three derelict houses left standing in Grahamsley Street. In Newcastle, Balmbra's was now the Carlton Hotel. Yet Clarence Walton, the *Gateshead Times* journalist, celebrated *Blaydon Races*.

> Wherever Geordies gather at home it is sung in a spirit of loyalty. Wherever they meet in far distant lands it serves to recall the coally Tyne, the ships that come and go, our famous bridges, the hardy, hospitable, industrious people who have proved their worth in the past, and upon whom the nation depends.

It was the 'national anthem of Tyneside'.[426] In 1949, T. & G. Allan printed *Lingford's High Level Tyneside Song Book* for the Bishop Auckland baking powder makers, to celebrate the bridge's centenary. It included *Blaydon Races* and *Cushie Butterfield*, but without its last verse.[427]

In 1951, William Robinson recorded *Blaydon Races*,[428] and Newcastle United won the FA Cup. In 1952, as United played for a place in the quarter finals, the 'unmistakable voice of the north' was 'raised exultantly' in its 'strains';[429] and United went on to win the trophy. The communist Albert Lancaster Lloyd edited *Come All Ye Bold Miners* for the National Coal Board and noted that a 'talented collier' had written *Blaydon Races*. It was the 'widest-renowned of all this kind of songs', but only 'By chance'.[430] Lloyd also edited *Coaldust Ballads* for the Workers' Music Association. He included *Cushie Butterfield*, but left out three verses, altered others and made several mistakes in his short note.

An old music hall song, evergreen in North-east England. Words by the collier-comedian George Ridley (1834-1864) who also wrote *Blaydon Races*. Tune adapted from the semi-traditional melody of *Polly Perkins*.[431]

Will Sahnow of the WMA arranged the tune for the piano.

'Cushie Butterfield' (A.L. Lloyd, Coaldust Ballads, 1952).

In 1953, Yale Music Corporation in London published Catcheside-Warrington's arrangements of five 'Tyneside Favourites', as sung by The Five Smith Brothers, a close harmony group from Tyneside.

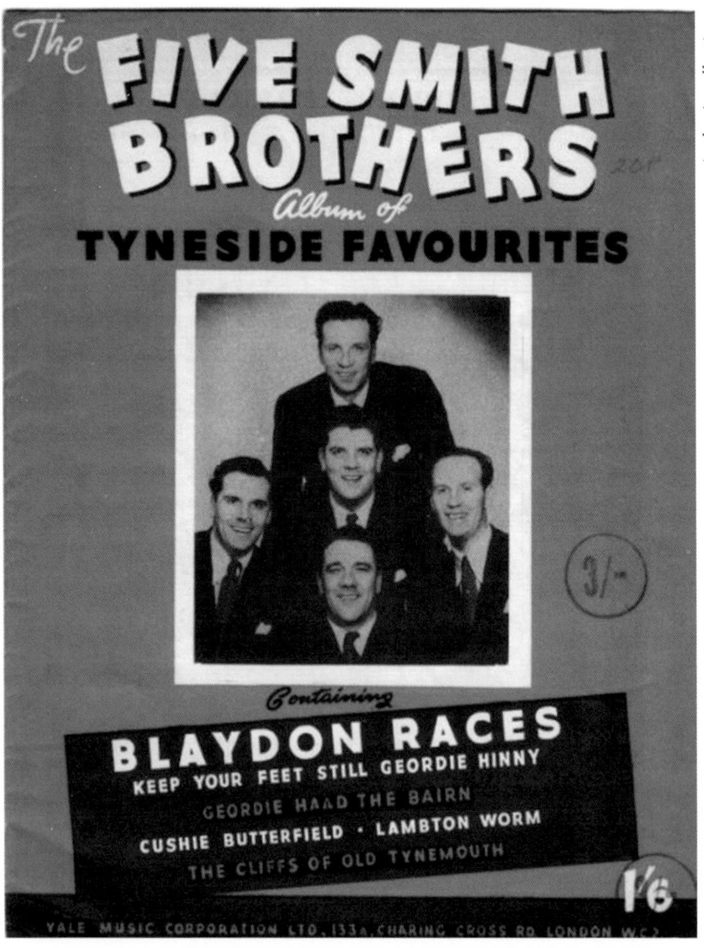

Author's collection

Vic Gammon's granny took him to see The Five Smith Brothers at the Brixton Empire in London, and *Blaydon Races* was their signature tune. They recorded it and *Cushie Butterfield* on a seven-inch, 45 revolutions per minute, Extended Play vinyl disc.

In 1955, *The Times* correctly predicted that if Newcastle United were winning in the FA Cup Final, 'we shall surely hear the voice of the north east raised in "The Blaydon races"'. In 1957, United got through to the fifth round, and 'there arose across the grey skies the thunderous echoes of *Blaydon Races*', but the match was drawn. The song burst out in the replay, but United lost. A 'spirited, if somewhat discordant, rendering' did not help Durham University's rugby team to win their championship.[432] Owen Brannigan, the 49-year-old Annitsford-born opera bass, recorded *Blaydon Races* on an EP.

In 1958, 1 Grahamsley Street was the last left standing and was about to become Regent Court flats. Clarence Walton's suggestion that the owners should 'affix an appropriate tablet' fell on deaf ears.[433] Around this time, Alec Forester recorded *Blaydon Races* and *Cushie Butterfield*, possibly in Sunderland. Neither was on the first EP in the Windmill Series of 'Geordie Dialect Records', and the 'Series' seems not to have continued.[434] In 1959, Clarence Walton wrote a *Preface* for T. & G. Allan's *Selection of Songs and Ballads of Northern England*, which aimed to 'serve as an introduction to a new edition of "Tyneside Songs"'. It included *Blaydon Races* and *Cushie Butterfield*, but without the final verse.[435] The new Tyne Tees Television company screened a 'test card' before programmes began each day, and played Arthur Wilkinson's three-minute 'Three Rivers Fantasy', which ended with *Blaydon Races*. Scottish and Newcastle Breweries commissioned a TV commercial and Owen Brannigan sang *The Blue Star Song* to the tune of *Cushie Butterfield*.

> If you want a beer that's perfection indeed,
> I'll give you a guide to fulfilling your need.
> At home by your fireside, in club or in bar,
> The sign of Good Taste is the famous Blue Star.

It's the strong beer, it's the bottled beer
With the North's biggest sale,
For complete satisfaction
Newcastle Brown Ale.

Yet Ridley's authorship of *Blaydon Races* came under scrutiny.

Joseph Hunter was born in 1807, the son of a Swalwell keelman. Around 1821, he became an apprentice chain-maker at Crowley's ironworks, but later moved to Carlisle. He returned to Tyneside by 1851, became a Wesleyan Methodist, worked in several places and ended as a tool burnisher at Armstrong's works. According to Thomas Menzies, who met him in 1886, Hunter claimed that he wrote *Gannin' to Blaydon Races*. The 'Elswick Poet' fell from a tram and died of his injuries in 1898;[436] yet in 1959, Hunter's granddaughter still believed that he wrote *Blaydon Races*.[437]

In 1960, Owen Brannigan recorded *Cushie Butterfield* on an EP. According to the *Gateshead Post*, it and, *The Sheels Lass for Me* were among the 'most popular songs' written by their 'immortal' author; but Reuben Brothers, the 'fancy goods dealers', occupied the site of 1 Grahamsley Street.[438] Around this time, Richard Ridley of 45 South Street, Gateshead, wrote to the *Gateshead Post*: 'Most of the Ridley family still reside in Gateshead and I have never heard of any of them having in their possession any cuttings or photographs of either George Ridley or Joseph Stephen Ridley', who he believed was his 'grandfather', and 'I think I am the only one with a portrait' of him.[439]

In 1961, the City & County of Newcastle upon Tyne 'in conjunction with' Blaydon Urban District Council – but not Gateshead Council – formed the Blaydon Races Centenary Joint Committee.[440] Councillor T. Leslie Cuthbertson of

Newcastle was its chair,[441] and there was a full-time organiser based in Ridley Place, Newcastle, by 1962.[442] In May, W.E. Hume, the Murton Branch Librarian, claimed that *Blaydon Races* – 'the work of an uneducated pitman and all the more credit to him for that' – was 'part of the national heritage'.[443]

The *Evening Chronicle* interviewed Jack Ridley, a retired staithsman, who lived in Larne Crescent, Sheriff Hill, Gateshead. He claimed that his 'father', Stephen Ridley, had become the 'one-mile champion of Great Britain', and completed the distance in four minutes and 20 seconds. Jack Ridley also claimed that he and his brother Richard, who was in 'an old man's home for the disabled', were 'the only surviving near relatives of Geordie Ridley'. His 'proudest possession' was 'an old-fashioned photographic portrait, showing his father holding the one-miler's belt'. Jack Ridley could not remember his father, who had died when he was 14, but Richard could. Jack Ridley's daughter, Mrs Hilda Henderson, had 'worked out from Stepehson Ridley senior's performance certificate' that he used 'one of his prizes of £100 to get married' but was 'unable to find out the real details of the family background'.[444] Stephenson Ridley senior's son, John, was born in 1883, and Richard in 1887, the year before his father's death.

The Blaydon Races Centenary Joint Committee's *Official Souvenir Brochure* cost one shilling, and included an advertisement by T. & G. Allan. Scottish & Newcastle Breweries claimed that their Brown Ale was 'As much a part of Tyneside' as *Blaydon Races*, and sponsored a City Hall concert involving Owen Brannigan, Ernest Lush, the Felling Male Voice Choir and the Northern Sinfonia Orchestra. By 'kind permission of United Breweries Ltd.', there would be a 'Civic Reception' for the 'Re-Opening of Old Tyme Music

Hall' at the Carlton Hotel, which was now refurbished as 'Balmbra's'. The Five Smith Brothers would star at a Grand Variety Concert in City Hall, supported by Newcastle police band and choir; and an 'Exiled Geordie's Dinner Dance' and 'Old Tyme Music Hall' would take place at the Black Bull in Blaydon, by 'kind permission of J.W. Cameron & Co. Ltd', the Hartlepool brewers. The winner of a brass band contest would receive the George Ridley Silver Trophy. The Chairman of Blaydon Urban District Council claimed that 'wherever Tynesiders have planted their feet' they sang *Blaydon Races* and the Lord Mayor of Newcastle hailed it as the 'Geordie Anthem'. Newcastle's Deputy City Librarian, William Tynemouth, noted that of all Ridley's songs, only *Blaydon Races* and *Cushie Butterfield* were 'heard regularly'.[445]

The Centenary events began on 2 June.[446] On 9 June, a quarter of a million people watched a parade costing £21,000,[447] as it went from Balmbra's to Blaydon, where there was 'galloping and sulky racing, open air dancing and a grand fireworks display'.[448] Crookhall Colliery Band

'Gan alang the Scotswood Road'. 9 June 1962.

won the £175 'golden trophy' and bands would compete for it annually in future.[449] Newcastle Corporation's 'condensed version' of the *Official Centenary Brochure* included illustrations from BBC TV's broadcast of Owen Brannigan's performance of *Blaydon Races*.[450] The leader of the Labour Party, Hugh Gaitskell, argued that the Centenary 'served to remind Geordies that they are Geordies at a time when they are in danger of being ironed out of existence by mass communications'.[451] Helen and Brian Mawson have a colour film of the events that shows him dancing.

Cecil Taylor's mother had grown up in Newcastle,[452] but he was born in Glasgow in 1929. He left school at 14 and worked as an electrician and then as a television engineer, but moved to Newcastle in 1955.[453] In 1962, he wrote his first play, *Aa Went to Blaydon Races*,[454] about the North East pitmen's bitter struggles with the coal owners.[455] Taylor worked as a travelling salesman for Clyde Factors, a Glasgow company that distributed gramophone records to J.G. Windows. Soon after, Maurice James Windows died aged 65.

In 1964, 15,000 'invaders' from Sunderland singing *Blaydon Races* inspired their team to draw with Manchester United. The 'battle hymn' accompanied another draw, but Sunderland lost the second replay. A 'knot of Newcastle supporters bellowed their "Blaydon Races" so proudly' as United beat Southampton. Tyne Tees TV screened *To See the Blaydon Races*.[456] In 1965, Frank Graham's *Tyneside Songs* included *Blaydon Races* and *Cushie Butterfield*, without its final verse.[457]

Brian Mawson recalls that he started working for J.G. Windows Ltd in 1960, at the age of 16. Alderson & Brentnall and J.G. Windows sold most Newcastle City Hall tickets and Brian helped to run the front of house for Windows' concerts. His colleague, the trombonist Ronnie

McLean, also asked him to take the money at the door on a Tuesday night at the New Orleans Jazz Club in Melbourne Street. In 1964, Owen Brannigan recorded *Blaydon Races* and *Cushie Butterfield* with the Consett Citizens' Choir for a 12-inch, 33-rpm, long-playing vinyl record. Brian knew how many copies of his EPs that Windows sold – Brannigan had bought some himself – but by 1966, EMI had deleted them. Brian decided to produce an LP of local songs with the local Decca rep, Ralph Smedley, who played percussion in a group called The Dombie Brothers with Joe Leatherland, a guitarist, and the singer, Michael Hunt. The recordings included *Cushie Butterfield*. Decca released the album in 1967. They paid Brian the handsome sum of £12 10s, and the album sold thousands. Owen Brannigan, Low Fell Ladies Choir, the Felling Male Voice Choir and the British Motor Corporation Concert Band, conducted by Harry Mortimer, recorded *Blaydon Races* and *Cushie Butterfield* in Gateshead Town Hall and EMI issued it on an LP. Newcastle Civic Centre's £21,000 Carillon Bells played the *Blaydon Races* chorus.[458]

In 1969, Brian Mawson, his Windows' colleague, Geraldine Wilkes, and the Birmingham distributor, Derek Wareham, registered Mawson & Wareham (Music) Ltd. For the second MWM LP in 1970, Roger Burgess adapted Scott Dobson's *Larn Yersel Geordie*, and BBC Look North presenters, Mike Neville and George House, performed it. MWM issued an album that used extracts from *Blaydon Races*, played by the Sunderland Youth International Concert Band, to introduce the 'Lessons'. Brian and Roger produced live shows at the Newcastle City Hall, which eventually became 'Geordierama'. One sketch about banking was entitled 'Cashier Butterfield', and the show always ended with the cast and audience singing *Blaydon Races*.

In 1970, Joan Gale published a history of Blaydon races.

> All over the world, exiled Geordies sing the ballad of 'The Blaydon Races'. In pubs and clubs and barrack rooms, at parties and football matches, wherever Geordies get together, this is the song that means home to them, the 'national anthem' of Tyneside. Americans, Australians, New Zealanders, Canadians, all know it, though they may never have been within a thousand miles of Blaydon, nor even realise that such a place really exists.

A 'modern glass and concrete town centre and a new dual carriageway' would replace much of the town centre. Gale could not find Ridley's grave, but 'Balmbra's' 'song and supper room' offered 'music hall entertainment typical of the Victorian era'.[459] Frank Graham's *Tyneside Songster* included *Blaydon Races* and what he called *Cushy Butterfield* from *Allan's Illustrated Tyneside Songs*, with 'slight alterations'; but he also called it *Cushie Butterfield*, and claimed that it was 'an anonymous work'.[460] Wallsend Youth Theatre performed *Aa went tae Blaydon Races* in the Guildhall.[461] Around this time, a T. & G. Allan Christmas card, 'With Best wishes from the North Country', featured the lyrics of *Blaydon Races*. It was 'probably' the 'most popular of all Tyneside Songs' and 'The National Anthem of Tyneside', but that was 'entirely due to its rollicking tune and chorus'.[462] Another Allan card included a drawing of a blowsy 'Cushie Butterfield' and a version of Ridley's lyrics. It claimed that *Blaydon Races* had 'ousted' *The Keel Row* 'from its place as the so called national anthem of Tyneside', and was 'sung all over the English speaking world'.[463] Michael Hunt recorded *Blaydon Races* for a Decca LP and the High Level Ranters recorded *Blaydon Races* and *Cushie Butterfield* for Trailer Records.

By 1971, there was a 'Geordie Ridley' pub in Blaydon town centre. In London, '1,500 Southerners' at a Lindisfarne concert 'clapped their hands in unison to the Geordie

National Anthem, *Blaydon Races*'.[464] In 1972, MWM issued a live recording of a 'Geordierama' show, which included a humorous rendition of *Cushie Butterfield* by The Shiremoor Marras, a group of miners and ex-miners who were part of The Northumbrian Traditional Group. Brian Mawson got a license from EMI to re-release Owen Brannigan's EPs and *Blaydon Races* and *Cushie Butterfield* from one of his LPs. Negotiations began with Brannigan, but the album appeared after he died in Newcastle's General Hospital in 1973. That year, Dave Harker's *George Ridley, Gateshead Poet and Vocalist* included all his surviving lyrics, and information supplied by Maurice Allan and Joseph Hutchinson. Frank Graham changed *George* to *Geordie* on the cover and added '*sings The Blaydon Races*', without consultation or consent.[465] Frank Manders, the Gateshead historian, noted that *Blaydon Races* was not Ridley's 'best-liked song in his own day', and repeated the 'legend' that, after he sang *Cushie Butterfield*, he 'had to escape irate members of the family' and Tom Gray.[466]

In 1974, the *Newcastle Journal* ran a competition for new lyrics for *Blaydon Races*. Five contestants won £2, and a composite version appeared as *The New Blaydon Races*; but one version was 'unprintable', and another noted the 'impending demise' of 'Blaydon Mechanics' Hall'.[467] In 1975, Alex Glasgow's third album for MWM included *Cushie Butterfield*, and was a great success. MWM and Newcastle's *Evening Chronicle* issued a Christmas album in support of the Sunshine Fund, which helped children with disabilities and their families. It included Owen Brannigan and the British Motor Corporation Concert Band's version of *Blaydon Races* and *Cushie Butterfield* by the High Level Ranters.

12 George Ridley's legacy

In 1976, Tyne and Wear County Council and Winlaton Local History Society put a plaque on the Blaydon Races Hotel, near Caroline Terrace, Blaydon, to commemorate the races on Stella Haughs.

In 1977, a Durham colliery band welcomed the US President Jimmy Carter by playing *Blaydon Races*;[468] but in 1978, A.L. Lloyd's revised edition of *Come All Ye Bold Miners* acknowledged that the song was the 'national anthem of the North East' by 'chance', and omitted it.[469] Mrs Hilda Henderson, of New Way, Clavering Park, Whickham, had a photograph of her 'grandfather', 'Joseph Stephen Ridley', with his prizes. She 'wondered if readers could trace the gold statuette' made by Northern Goldsmiths of Newcastle to commemorate the centenary of *Blaydon Races* and hoped it would go to Shipley Art Gallery on permanent loan.[470] In 1979, the Tyneside comedian Bobby Thompson was at the Old Vic in London, and forgot to tell the musical director that he wanted to sing *Blaydon Races*, but several members of the orchestra were originally from Tyneside and 'produced a perfect version from memory'.[471] MWM reissued the 1950s EMI recordings by The Five Smith Brothers, which included *Blaydon Races* and *Cushie Butterfield*.

In 1982 Alan Price, a former member of The Animals group, recorded *Cushie Butterfield* and *Blaydon Races* for an MWM LP that fellow 'Animal', Chas Chandler, produced in his Portland Studios, Portland Place, London. *Blaydon Races* was also used on MWM's 'Newcastle United Souvenir Album' in 1984. After the demolition of the Blaydon Races Hotel, the plaque was relocated in Stella Road.

In 1985, Little Billy Fane recorded an LP of Tyneside Music Hall songs. David Haslam arranged the music and conducted the 'pit orchestra' and the album included *Blaydon Races*, *Cushie Butterfield* and *Shields Lass for Me*. Barry Boyd, the promotions manager at Newcastle's *Evening Chronicle*, asked MWM to organise a prestigious musical event to celebrate the paper's centenary. David Haslam and the Northern Sinfonia Orchestra organised 'An Evening of Songs of Northumbria' at Newcastle City Hall and Haslam arranged a number of northern songs for Thomas Allen and Sheila Armstrong. The concert was a great success. Recordings took place in All Saints Church, Newcastle, in 1987, with Thomas Allen, Sheila Armstrong and the Northern Sinfonia Orchestra and Chorus. MWM issued an LP, a cassette and their first CD, which culminated in a rousing version of *Blaydon Races*.

In the early 1990s, a *Blaydon Races* plaque appeared in Blaydon.

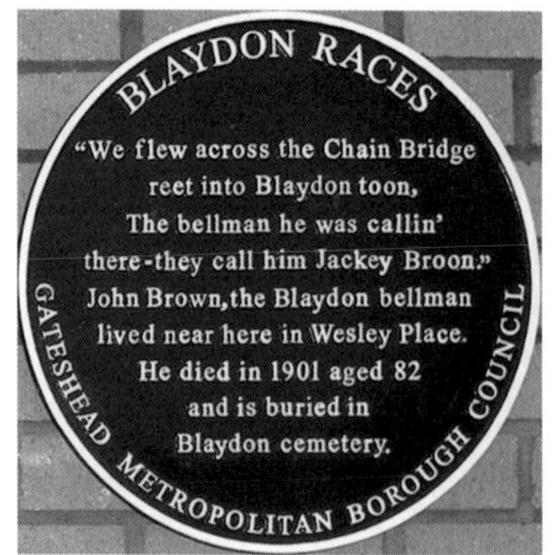

In 1992, Channel 4 TV and Yorkshire TV asked the award-winning director, Geoff Wonfor and MWM to produce a film using the recording session at All Saints Church, Newcastle.

David Haslam arranged local songs, including *Cushie Butterfield*. Another performance took place in 1993 at Durham Cathedral, to mark the 900th anniversary of its foundation. Channel 4 screened the film nationally as part of their Christmas build up, and *Radio Times* made it one of their 'Choices'. A VHS video included *Cushie Butterfield* and ended with the cathedral performance of *Blaydon Races*. In 1994, Yorkshire TV and Tyne Tees TV screened the film.

In 1995, Gateshead Metropolitan Borough Council put a plaque on the Grahamsley Street side of the William IV in High Street.

MWM's license for 'Owen Brannigan's Northumbria' had

Jenifer Maughan, Gateshead Libraries

The Willian IV pub Gateshead.

expired in the 1980s, but there was still a demand for his recordings in the 1990s. In 1998, to coincide with what would have been Brannigan's 90th birthday, MWM bought the rights to the album. The master tapes included spoken introductions by Brannigan, which had not been on the original LP, and the whole recording formed the basis of the new CD. Some popular songs were missing, including *Cushie Butterfield* and *Blaydon Races*, so Graeme Danby, the Consett-born principle bass at the English National Opera, recorded them with the Brown Ale Brass Band. MWM acquired Scottish and Newcastle Breweries' Brown Ale TV commercial that Brannigan made in 1959, and three unused commercials using other tunes, including *Blaydon Races*, were on the CD, which celebrated 70 years of Newcastle Brown Ale. The commercial film has not been found.

In 2000, *Blaydon Races* introduced the Sunday for Sammy Trust's shows at Newcastle City Hall, which funded grants for talented North East performers. In 2001, MWM issued an album of songs, which Denis Weatherley had sung in Gateshead Town Hall in the 1950s, accompanied by Clifton Helliwell on piano. The recordings were digitally remastered and carefully restored by Frank Wappat, and included *Cushie Butterfield*. Owen Brannigan's *Blaydon Races* appeared on CD. In 2002, with the help of a grant from New Labour government's Heritage Lottery, MWM issued the 'Northumbria Anthology' boxed set of 20 CDs. They included almost 300 tracks by a vast array of performers in folk, rock, classical and traditional styles. Around half came from MWM's back catalogue, including *Blaydon Races* by Tom Allen and Sheila Armstrong, *Sheels Lass for Me* by Billy Fane and *Cushie Butterfield* by Tom Allen. David Haslam gave *The Bobby Cure* a new tune and arranged the lyrics for the speaker and the Brown Ale Brass Band accompanied the project's researcher, Johnny Handle.

The Marriott hotel group owned William Irving's painting, *Blaydon Races*, and displayed it at the Gosforth Park Hotel. When they put it up for auction at Sotheby's in London, they expected to get £60,000, so the Heritage Lottery Fund, Gateshead Metropolitan Borough Council, private trusts and donors raised a fighting fund for Tyne & Wear Museums. They paid £124,000 for it, including fees, 'because of its regional importance rather than its artistic merit', and displayed it at Shipley Art Gallery in Gateshead.[472]

In 2004, Alan Clarke of Dire Straits arranged an instrumental version of *Blaydon Races* for the Sunday for Sammy show. MWM filmed it and donated the proceeds to the Trust. The Folk Archive Research North East website published the printed lyrics of most of George Ridley's songs,[473] and Keith Gregson's 'Ridley, George [Geordy]', appeared in the *Oxford Dictionary of National Biography*.[474]

In summer 2005, there was a series of sporting, artistic and musical events in Blaydon. The New Labour Local Heritage Initiative provided money via One North East and the Single Regeneration Budget to pay for Ken Irving's painting of characters and scenes from Ridley's song. The Single Regeneration Budget and the Community Foundation paid £6,500 for Tom Ward's mural in Blaydon Precinct. On 9 June, four thousand runners, singing *Blaydon Races*, began the 25th Nike-sponsored Blaydon Race from Newcastle.[475] The Local Heritage Initiative, Heritage Lottery Fund, Countryside Agency and Nationwide Building Society sponsored the 'Blaydon Races Heritage Trail' booklet. It described the people and places in Ridley's song, and claimed that he was 'remembered for two classic Tyneside songs: *Cushy Butterfield*, the Tyneside fish lass who liked her beer' – evidently confusing it with Ned Corvan's *The Cullercoats*

Fish Lass – and 'the now world famous *Blaydon Races*'.[476] Museums, Libraries and Archives Renaissance North East, Tyne & Wear Archives Connecting Through Culture, the Department for Culture Media and Sport, Gateshead Metropolitan Borough Council and the Heritage Lottery Fund sponsored a Tyne & Wear Museums 'Learning Pack' for teachers, which focused on Irving's *Blaydon Races*.[477]

One hundred and forty or so years after George Ridley's death, a small black stone, with gold lettering and a sketch of him as 'Johnny Luik-Up', marked his grave in Gateshead East Cemetery, and directions appeared on the web.

> As you enter the cemetery from Cemetery Walk take the path on your right, keeping the Church to your right, proceed approximately 50 metres, then follow the path to the left at the junction. Half way along, leave this path taking a left turn 20 metres into the plot lies the new stone commemorating the burial site of George Ridley. The inscription on the grave reads '*In Memory of George Ridley. Composer of The Blaydon Races. Born at Gateshead died 11th Sept, 1864 aged 30 years*'.[478]

Ridley was 29 when he died on 9 September 1864.

Around 2005, DAV Developments bought Balmbra's. It remained closed for two years,[479] and then became a nightclub. In 2007, the Houghton Weavers' versions of *Blaydon Races* and *Cushie Butterfield* appeared on *20 Folk Classics*. In 2008, to celebrate the centenary of his birth, MWM issued a DVD called 'The Owen Brannigan Story – A Tribute by Graeme Danby'. Danby sang two versions of *Blaydon Races*; one with a huge choir at the Sage, Gateshead, and another with the crowd at St James' Park, Newcastle, at half time. He also recreated the Brown Ale TV commercial at the Bridge Hotel, Newcastle, with Northumbria University students as the audience. MWM had always wanted to issue a contemporary rendition of *Blaydon Races*, and Steve Daggett and Paul Campbell had arranged the backing track years before. In 2009, MWM issued a DVD called 'Sir Bobby Robson – A Knight to Remember'. It included his final interview, and the rock version of *Blaydon Races*, sung by *Auf Wiedersehen Pet* stars Jimmy Nail, Tim Healy and Kevin Whately, with Billy Mitchell's new final verse.

And now a word for Bobby Robson, hero of the Toon;
A football man, a gentleman, who never let we doon;
A friendly word, a cheery smile, and brave right to the end;
We're proud to say you're one of ours, Sir Bob, Auf Wiedershen.

The DVD raised money for the Sir Bobby Robson Foundation, which supports cancer research. This version of *Blaydon Races* is available Youtube,[480] as is the Royal Regiment of Fusiliers band's rendition of the tune.[481]

In 2010, a Gateshead Metropolitan Borough Council leaflet about Blaydon races acknowledged the 'kind permission' of T. & G. Allan for quoting Ridley's song.[482] Keith Gregson heard a riverside pianist in San Antonio, Texas playing a version of *Blaydon Races*, which he had 'picked up from touring rugby players in Canada twenty years ago'. Only 'about half the words and half the tune were accurate', but he 'gave it some welly and it was well received'.In 2011, MWM issued a documentary presented by Eric Robson and Charlie Hardwick, directed by Geoff Wonfor and produced by Ray Laidlaw. It included *Blaydon Races* from the Bobby Robson DVD.

DAV Developments owned and operated care homes across the North East and had substantial property investments across the country, employing 450 people. The company owned two pubs, Pumphrey's and Balmbra's, in Newcastle's Cloth Market, and the Attic bar in Mosley Street, and had paid £5 million for Nos. 3, 5, 7, 9 and 11

Grey Street.[483] They wanted to spend up to £15 million more to build a 55-bed luxury hotel on the sites. According to the planning application, 'The Dorchester of the North' would have 'at least four restaurants', including one on the roof, and entrances in Grey Street, Mosley Street and Cloth Market.[484] The 'former music hall', Balmbra's, would be 'a function suite for weddings and corporate events'.[485] DAV management were 'not sure of the exact plans', but 'all its historic features' of what had recently been a dance hall would 'remain intact'. (The Balmbra's Music Saloon where Ridley had sung had burned down completely in 1899.) Up to spring 2012, DAV had 'forgotten about the anniversary' of *Blaydon Races*, but would be happy to allow Balmbra's to reopen as a bar for the occasion.[486]

Today, you can still hear the chorus, if not the verses, of George Ridley's best-known song when Newcastle United are playing at home or away; and the Carillon Bells of Newcastle Civic Centre ring out its chorus tune as jerkily as ever.

References

[1] Population figures and personal information are from the census
[2] Mackenzie 1827: 749
[3] Simpson 1998 – I owe this reference to Peter Jefferies
[4] Allan Papers
[5] Manders 1973: 18, 53, 162, 178
[6] Allan 1872: *facing* 17
[7] Gregson 2004
[8] Allan Papers
[9] www.flickr.com/photos/davewebster14/2463451927/
[10] Manders 1973: 58
[11] www.mininginstitute.org.uk/library/bell/6.htm
[12] Allan Papers
[13] Greenwell 1888: 5-6
[14] Burt 1924: 5
[15] Allan Papers
[16] Challinor & Ripley 1968: 60-131
[17] *York Herald* 1 Jun 1844
[18] www.mininginstitute.org.uk/library/bell/6.htm
[19] Harker 1999: 41-66
[20] www.dmm.org.uk/colliery/t025.htm
[21] Allan Papers
[22] Cooter 2005: 22
[23] *Newcastle Journal* 13 Jan 1849
[24] *Newcastle Guardian* 13 Jan 1849
[25] Anon 1891: 554
[26] Hume 1854
[27] Manders 1973: 183
[28] Fane 1985: 14
[29] *Newcastle Courant* 22 Sep 1854, 7 Dec 1855, 21 Mar 1856, 2, 16 Apr 1858
[30] Allan Papers
[31] Allan 1872: *facing* 17
[32] Manders 1973: 165
[33] *Newcastle Guardian* 8 Jun 1850
[34] www.genuki.org.uk/big/eng/NBL/Cholera/index.html
[35] *Newcastle Guardian* 9 Sep 1854
[36] Map of Gateshead, Gateshead Libraries
[37] *Newcastle Courant* 28 Mar, 25 Jul 1858, 25 Nov 1859
[38] *Newcastle Courant* 27 Jul 1860

[39] Allan 1872: *facing* 17
[40] Allan Papers
[41] Allan 1872: *facing* 17
[42] *Newcastle Courant* 21 Oct 1864
[43] *Newcastle Courant* 27 Nov 1840
[44] *The Era* 27 Feb, 3 Apr 1842, 16 Jul, 13 Aug 1843, 30 Jun 1844, 26 Jan 1845
[45] Robson 1870: 15-16
[46] *Newcastle Journal* 27 Jun 1846
[47] *Newcastle Courant* 23 Oct 1846
[48] Robson 1854: 8-10
[49] 1841 Newcastle Directory
[50] Harker 1985: 31-2, 35
[51] 1845 and 1847 Newcastle Directories
[52] *The Era* 16, 23 Nov, 14 Dec 1862
[53] *Newcastle Guardian* 15 May 1847
[54] Allan 1872: *facing* page 16
[55] *Newcastle Guardian* 15 May 1847
[56] *The Era* 26 Dec 1847, 27 Aug 1848
[57] *Newcastle Courant* 16, 22 Dec 1848
[58] *The Era* 25 Mar 1849
[59] *Newcastle Journal* 15 Dec 1849
[60] *The Era* 24 Feb, 17 Mar, 19 May, 6 Oct, 24 Nov, 1, 15 Dec 1850
[61] *Newcastle Journal* 29 Jun 1850
[62] *The Era* 10, 24 Feb, 17 Mar, 19 May, 6 Oct, 24 Nov, 1, 15 Dec 1850
[63] Anon undated
[64] *The Era* 6 Apr, 5 Oct, 30 Nov 1851
[65] *Newcastle Guardian* 27 Dec 1851
[66] Rewcastle 1854: 1, 4-6, 10
[67] *The Era* 30 Nov 1851, 7 Mar, 13 Jun, 22, 29 Aug 1852, 13 Nov, 18 Dec 1853
[68] *Newcastle Guardian* 7 Apr 1855
[69] *The Era* 1 Jul 1855, 6 Apr 1856, 11 Jan 1857
[70] *Newcastle Journal* 7 Mar 1857
[71] *Newcastle Guardian* 21 Nov 1857
[72] *The Era* 6 Dec 1857
[73] *Newcastle Journal* 19 Dec 1857
[74] *Newcastle Courant* 25 Mar 1859
[75] 1859 Newcastle Directory
[76] Reed 1903: 195-6
[77] 1834, 1838, 1839, 1844, 1847, 1850 Newcastle Directories

[78] *Newcastle Guardian* 6 Jul, 26 Oct 1850, 31 May 1851
[79] 1852, 1855 Newcastle Directories
[80] *Newcastle Journal* 25 Oct 1856
[81] Adams 1903: 474
[82] 1857 and 1859 Newcastle Directories
[83] *The Era* 1, 22 Jan, 25 Nov 1860
[84] *Newcastle Daily Chronicle* 20 Dec 1860
[85] *Newcastle Courant* 26 Dec 1873
[86] Allen 2007: 18-19
[87] *Newcastle Courant* 26 Dec 1873
[88] Allen 2007: 20, 22-4, 41-2, 44, 53-5
[89] Todd 1991: 38-9
[90] Allen 2007: 45, 55
[91] Todd 1991: 37
[92] Allen 2007: 45
[93] Todd 1991: 37
[94] Allen 2007: 56, 60
[95] Todd 1991: 18, 28-9, 42-3, 50-1
[96] *The Era* 2 Jun 1861
[97] Gale 1970: 5, 16, 18
[98] *Newcastle Daily Chronicle* 18, 21 May, 19, 27 Jun 5, 9, 16, 23, 30 Jul 1861
[99] Dixon 1987: 13
[100] Fane 1985: 29
[101] Allan 1873: 20
[102] *The Era* 28 Jul 1861
[103] Allan Papers
[104] Allan Papers
[105] Corvan 1854: 18-21
[106] *Newcastle Weekly Chronicle* 20 Sep 1877, 20 Sep 1879
[107] https://jscholarship.library.jhu.edu/handle/1774.2/22904
[108] Allan Papers
[109] Allan 1862: 17
[110] Allan Papers
[111] *Newcastle Weekly Chronicle* 29 Sep 1877
[112] Heslop 1892, Volume 1: 128-9
[113] Allan 1873: 19
[114] Allan Papers
[115] Allan Papers
[116] *The Era* 19 Feb 1898
[117] *Newcastle Courant* 7 Dec 1862, 27 Sep 1867

[118] *The Era* 19 Feb 1898
[119] Barker 1983: 63
[120] *Newcastle Courant* 22 Sep 1861, 27 Sep 1867
[121] *Newcastle Guardian* 28 Jul 1860
[122] *Newcastle Journal* 10 Nov 1860, 22 Jun 1861
[123] *Newcastle Daily Chronicle* 23 Jul, 5, 9, 12 Aug 1861
[124] *Newcastle Journal* 26, 29, 30 Aug 1861
[125] *Newcastle Guardian* 31 Aug 1861
[126] *Newcastle Courant* 13 Sep 1861
[127] *Newcastle Guardian* 14 Sep 1861
[128] *Newcastle Courant* 22 Sep 1861
[129] *Newcastle Guardian* 21 Sep 1861
[130] *Newcastle Daily Chronicle* 7, 24, 28, 30 Oct 1861
[131] *The Era* 13 Sep 1874
[132] *The Era* 1 Dec 1850, 24, 31 Dec 1854, 6 Apr, 3 Aug, 9 Nov 1856.
[133] *The Era* 11 Oct, 15, 22 Nov 1857, 21 Mar, 5 Sep 1858, 4 Aug, 13 Oct, 29 Dec 1861
[134] French 2005: 13
[135] Allan 1891: 341-2
[136] Allan 1891: 506-7
[137] Bell and Paterson 1969: *unpaginated*
[138] *Newcastle Courant* 31 May 1850, 11 Jan 1856, 5 Feb 1869
[139] *Newcastle Daily Chronicle* 4, 11 Nov 1861
[140] Nicholson 1890: 110-14
[141] *Newcastle Guardian* 21 Nov 1868; *Newcastle Courant* 19 Jan 1877, 17 Jan 1879
[142] *Shields Daily Gazette* 16 Mar 1901
[143] Allan 1873: 31
[144] **https://jscholarship.library.jhu.edu/handle/1774.2/30452**
[145] *Newcastle Journal* 12 Nov 1861; *Newcastle Courant* 15 Nov 1861; *Newcastle Guardian* 16 Nov 1861
[146] Adams 1903: 480
[147] Todd 1991: 57
[148] *Newcastle Daily Chronicle* 12, 13 Nov,
[149] *Newcastle Courant* 29 Nov 1861
[150] *Newcastle Courant* 24 Nov 1861
[151] *Newcastle Daily Chronicle* 2, 9 Dec 1861
[152] *The Era* 15 Dec 1861
[153] *Newcastle Courant* 15 Dec 1861
[154] *Newcastle Daily Chronicle* 16, 17, 19 Dec 1861
[155] *Newcastle Guardian* 28 Dec 1861; *Newcastle Daily Journal* 28 Dec 1861

[156] *The Era* 29 Dec 1861
[157] *Newcastle Daily Chronicle* 6, 10, 12, 13 Jan 1862
[158] Fynes 1971: 195-206
[159] *The Era* 2 Feb 1862
[160] *Newcastle Courant* 19 Feb 1862
[161] *Newcastle Daily Chronicle* 1, 3, 19 Feb 1862
[162] *Newcastle Journal* 19 Feb 1862
[163] Todd 1991: 62
[164] *Newcastle Daily Chronicle* 7, 8 Apr, 31 May, 5, 6 Jun 1862
[165] Tynemouth 1962a: 54
[166] Gale 1970: 19
[167] *Newcastle Daily Chronicle* 9, 10 Jun 1862
[168] Tynemouth 1962a: 53
[169] **www.tynefolk.co.uk/folk-articles.php**
[170] American Antiquarian Society, Ballads 058t 04
[171] New*castle* Library cutting
[172] *Newcastle Daily Journal* 19 Jul 1862
[173] *Newcastle Daily Chronicle* 8, 21 Jul 1862
[174] *Newcastle Courant* 27 Jul 1862
[175] *The Era* 31 Aug, 21 Sep, 12, 19 Oct, 9 Nov 1862
[176] Allan 1873: 22
[177] *Newcastle Courant* 2 Jun 1882
[178] *The Era* 18 Oct 1857
[179] Bennett 1986: 5
[180] Tynemouth 1962a: 56
[181] Gammon 2008: 146, 163
[182] *Newcastle Daily Chronicle* 21 Oct 1862; *Newcastle Journal* 21 Oct1862; *Newcastle Daily Journal* 25 Oct 1862; *Newcastle Courant* 31 Oct 1862
[183] *Newcastle Daily Chronicle* 12 Sep 1864
[184] Allan Correspondence
[185] Hutchinson Correspondence
[186] 1811 Newcastle Directory
[187] *Newcastle Courant* 15 Aug 1829, 30 Jul 1831, 4 Apr 1835
[188] Allan Correspondence
[189] Allan Correspondence
[190] Hutchinson Correspondence
[191] Allan Papers
[192] Mackenzie 1827: 450-1
[193] Allan Papers
[194] Mackenzie 1827: 446, 451

[195] Allan Papers
[196] Clarke 1979: 3-6, 9
[197] Allan Papers
[198] Allan 1891: 322-3
[199] *Newcastle Courant* 27 Aug 1847
[200] Allan 1891: 323
[201] Clarke 1979: 4, 10
[202] Allan's 'Hawthorn's Cheps' in the *Newcastle Weekly Chronicle* has not been traced
[203] Hutchinson Correspondence
[204] 1858, 1859 and 1861 Newcastle Directories
[205] Hutchinson Correspondence
[206] Hunt 1975: 29
[207] Allan Papers
[208] Harker 1986: 117
[209] Allan 1862: 17-22, 28-9, 31-2, 47-8, 65-7, 68-9, 71-2, 73-6
[210] Allan Papers
[211] Jensen 2002
[212] *Newcastle Courant* 7 Dec 1862
[213] *Newcastle Daily Chronicle* 7 Dec 1862
[214] Todd 1991: 68
[215] *Newcastle Daily Chronicle* 7 Dec 1862
[216] Hutchinson Correspondence
[217] 1863 Newcastle Directory
[218] *The Era* 11 Jan 1863
[219] *Newcastle Guardian* 18 Apr 1863; *Newcastle Daily Journal* 22 Apr 1863
[220] *The Era* 14 Jun, 12, 19 Jul, 23 Aug 1863
[221] *Shields Gazette* 11 Jun 1955
[222] Allan 1891: 528
[223] *Newcastle Daily Chronicle* 5, 10, 12 Oct 1863
[224] *Newcastle Daily Journal* 21 Oct 1863
[225] *The Era* 25 Oct 1863
[226] *Newcastle Guardian* 24 Oct 1863
[227] *Newcastle Daily Chronicle* 24, 26 Oct 1863
[228] *Newcastle Daily Journal* 16 Jan 1864
[229] Heslop 1896: 30
[230] *Newcastle Courant* 25 Sep 1885
[231] *The Era* 19, 26 Jan 1862, 20 Sep 1863
[232] *Newcastle Daily Chronicle* 21 Dec 1863
[233] *The Era* 10, 17, 24, 31 Jan 1864

[234] *Newcastle Guardian* 13 Feb 1864
[235] *Newcastle Courant* 12 Feb 1864
[236] *The Era* 3 Apr 1864
[237] Allan Papers
[238] *Newcastle Daily Chronicle* 7 Jun, 18 Jul 1864
[239] Allan 1872: *facing* 17
[240] Allan Papers
[241] *Newcastle Daily Chronicle* 12 Sep 1864
[242] Allan 1864: 17-22, 28-9, 31-2, 65-7, 68-9, 71-2, 73-6
[243] Heslop 1896: 30
[244] 1865 Newcastle Directory
[245] Todd 1991: 80
[246] Death Certificate
[247] Allan 1865: 17-22, 28-9, 31-2, 65-7, 68-9, 71-2, 73-6
[248] 1865 Newcastle Directory
[249] *Newcastle Courant* 13 Oct 1865
[250] *The Era* 17 Dec 1865
[251] *Newcastle Courant* 19 Jan 1866, 27 Sep 1867
[252] *Newcastle Guardian* 6 Oct 1866
[253] Barker 1983: 64-5
[254] *Newcastle Guardian* 2 Feb 1867
[255] 1867 Newcastle Directory
[256] *The Era* 16, 30 Jun, 15, 22 Sep 1867
[257] *Newcastle Courant* 20 Sep 1867
[258] Todd 1991: 66-7
[259] *The Era* 26 Sep 1867
[260] *Newcastle Daily Chronicle* 24 Sep, 5 Dec 1867
[261] Allen 2007: 90
[262] Todd 1991: 68
[263] *Newcastle Courant* 6 Mar, 30 Oct 1868
[264] Tilly 2010: 124-5
[265] 1869, 1870 and 1873 Newcastle Directories.
[266] Hutchinson Correspondence
[267] Gale 1970: 29
[268] 1871 Newcastle Directory
[269] Hutchinson Correspondence
[270] Harker 1986: 116-21
[271] Allan Papers
[272] Allan 1891: 513-15
[273] Newberry Library, Chicago
[274] Harrison 1872

[275] Allan 1891: 515-17
[276] Tynemouth 1962a: 56
[277] Allan 1872: 17-22, 28-9, 31-2, 65-9, 71-6, 184-5, 192-3, 200-1, 205-7, 220-1
[278] *Newcastle Guardian* 16 Apr 1870
[279] *Newcastle Guardian* 4 Feb 1854
[280] *Sheffield Daily Telegraph* 14 Oct 1868
[281] *Newcastle Guardian* 20 Mar 1869
[282] *Sheffield Independent* 2 Jan 1871
[283] *Newcastle Courant* 17 Mar 1871
[284] *Penny Illustrated Paper* 20 Jan 1872
[285] *Newcastle Guardian* 29 Jun 1872
[286] *Sheffield Daily Telegraph* 8 Jul 1872
[287] *Newcastle Guardian* 10 Aug 1872
[288] Manders 1973: 253-4
[289] *Sheffield Daily Telegraph* 13 Oct 1873; *Newcastle Courant* 17 Oct 1873; *Lloyd's Weekly Paper* 19 Oct 1873
[290] Manders 1973: 117
[291] Wilson 1873
[292] Allan Papers
[293] Allan 1873: 17-24, 31-2, 63-9, 184-5, 192-3, 200-1, 205-7, 220-1
[294] *Newcastle Courant* 22 Mar 1872, 26 Dec 1873
[295] Todd 1991: 115-20
[296] 1874 Newcastle Directory
[297] Hunt 1975: 94
[298] Hutchinson Correspondence
[299] Harker 1986: 121
[300] Wilson 1874
[301] *Newcastle Courant* 9 Oct 1874
[302] Allan 1874: 17-24, 31-2, 63-9, 184-5, 192-3, 200-1, 205-7, 220-1
[303] Allan Papers
[304] Wilson 1890: xxxii
[305] *The Era* 1 Feb 1875
[306] *Newcastle Daily Chronicle* 15, 16, 18, 24 Feb 1875
[307] Allan Papers
[308] *Newcastle Weekly Chronicle* 20 Sep 1877
[309] *Newcastle Courant* 22 Dec 1876
[310] Newcastle Library cutting
[311] *The Era* 11, 18 Feb 1877
[312] 1877 Newcastle Directory
[313] Allan Correspondence

[314] *Newcastle Weekly Chronicle* 29 Sep 1879
[315] 1881 Newcastle Directory
[316] *Newcastle Weekly Chronicle* 7 Jan, 31 May, 19 Aug 1882
[317] *Newcastle Weekly Courant* 25 Sep 1885
[318] Hutchinson Correspondence
[319] 1886 and 1887 Newcastle Directories
[320] Milne 1971: 69-70
[321] Todd 1991: 126, 128
[322] Allen 2007: 103
[323] Todd 1991: 136, 144-7, 159
[324] Allen 2007: 141-2
[325] Todd 1991: 158, 162
[326] Gale 1970: 31-2
[327] 1890 Newcastle Directory
[328] Wilson 1890: xv
[329] Allan Papers
[330] Hutchinson Correspondence
[331] Allan Papers
[332] Allan 1891: 449-63
[333] Hutchinson Correspondence
[334] *Newcastle Weekly Courant* 11 Jun 1892
[335] Hutchinson Correspondence
[336] Hutchinson Correspondence
[337] Hutchinson Correspondence
[338] 1894 Newcastle Directory
[339] *Newcastle Courant* 8 Jun 1895
[340] *Edinburgh Evening News* 14 Feb 1898; *The Era* 19 Feb 1898
[341] Hutchinson Correspondence
[342] www.arthurlloyd.co.uk/Newcastle/BalmbrasMusicHallNewcastle.htm
[343] Hall 1996: 31-2
[344] *Newcastle Courant* 9 Jun 1900
[345] Todd 1991: 164
[346] Hall 1996: 32
[347] *Sunderland Daily Echo* 11 Apr 1900
[348] www.bpears.org.uk/Misc/Gateshead_Plaques/#BlaydonRaces2
[349] www.arthurlloyd.co.uk/Newcastle/BalmbrasMusicHallNewcastle.htm
[350] Hutchinson Correspondence
[351] Hall 1996: 31-2
[352] Hall 1996: 32-3
[353] Tynemouth 1962a: 51
[354] Gale 1970: 36

[355] Allan Correspondence
[356] Hutchinson Correspondence
[357] 1841 Newcastle Directory
[358] **catchietribalpagescom/**
[359] *Newcastle Courant* 4 Feb 1848
[360] 1850 Newcastle Directory
[361] *Newcastle Courant* 24 Jan, 20 Jun 1851
[362] **catchietribalpagescom/**
[363] *Newcastle Courant* 1 Dec 1854, 5 Mar 1858, 2 Mar 1860, 8 Mar 1861, 8 Mar 1867, 6 Mar 1868, 28 Apr 1882, 18 May, 17 Aug, 28 Sep 1883, 14 Mar, 9 May 1884, 7 Aug, 25 Sep 1885, 11 Mar 1887
[364] **catchietribalpagescom/**
[365] *The Era* 21 Jan 1872,
[366] *Newcastle Courant* 6 May 1877
[367] *The Era* 23 Nov 1889,
[368] *Sunderland Daily Echo* 4 Aug 1891
[369] **catchietribalpagescom/**
[370] Stephenson 1999: 9
[371] *The Era* 14, 21 Feb 1891
[372] Stephenson 1999: 9
[373] *The Era* 7 Feb, 7 Nov 1891
[374] *Sunderland Daily Echo* 11 Feb 1892
[375] *Newcastle Weekly Courant* 13 Feb 1892
[376] *Sunderland Daily Echo* 27 Feb 1892
[377] *The Era* 16 Apr, 14 May 1892
[378] Stephenson 1999: 9, 24
[379] *The Era* 7, 28 Jan, 18, 25 Feb, 4, 11, 18, 25 Mar, 8, 15, 22 Apr, 3 Jun, 15 Jul, 2, 9, 23, 30 Sep, 7, 14, 21, 28 Oct, 4, 25 Nov, 9, 23 Dec 1893
[380] Stephenson 1981: 21
[381] Stephenson 1999: 9-11, 33
[382] *The Era* 20 Jan, 3, 17 Feb, 7 Apr, 26 May, 9, 16, 23, 30 Jun, 18 Aug
[383] *Dundee Courier* 21 Aug 1894
[384] *The Era* 29 Sep, 13, 20, 27 Oct, 24 Nov, 1, 8 Dec 1894, 23 Feb, 9, 16, 30 Mar, 6, 27 Apr, 4, 11, 18, 25 May, 1, 8, 15, 22 Jun, 13, 27 Jul, 10, 17, 24, 31 Aug, 14, 21, 28 Sep, 5, 12, 26 Oct, 9, 23 Nov, 14, 21, 28 Dec 1895, 4, 11, 25 Jan, 8, 15, 22 Feb, 7, 14, 21 Mar, 4 Apr, 9, 16 May 1896
[385] Stephenson 1999: 6, 8, 12
[386] Stephenson 1983: 45-6
[387] *The Era* 18 Dec 1892
[388] *The Era* 8 Sep 1900
[389] *Shields Daily Gazette* 26 Nov 1901

[390] I owe this point to Ray Stephenson
[391] Stephenson 1999: 30
[392] Stephenson Undated CD A
[393] Stephenson 1999: 17
[394] Stephenson 1999: 41
[395] Catcheside-Warrington 1911: 1, 3
[396] Catcheside-Warrington 1927: 3-5
[397] Catcheside-Warrington 1911: 5, 12-13, 18-19
[398] Catcheside-Warrington 1912
[399] Gale 1970: 36
[400] Catcheside-Warrington 1913
[401] Allan Correspondence
[402] I owe this point to Ray Stephenson
[403] Tynemouth 1962a: 52
[404] Gale 1970: 51-4
[405] Stephenson 1999: 14, 18, 20, 30
[406] *The Times* 28 Mar 1924
[407] Catcheside-Warrington 1924
[408] Catcheside-Warrington 1927: cover, 3-5, 12-13, 18-19, 26, 29
[409] *The Times* 9 Jul 1927
[410] Stephenson 1999: 22, 27-9
[411] Stephenson Undated CD A
[412] Stephenson 1999: 21-2, 27
[413] Stephenson Undated CD A
[414] Stephenson Undated CD B
[415] Stephenson 1999: 43
[416] Catcheside-Warrington 1927 and 1929a, b and c
[417] Manders 1973: 173
[418] Stephenson 1999: 42
[419] Stephenson 1983: 45
[420] Newcastle Library cutting
[421] I owe this point to Ray Stephenson
[422] Stephenson 1999: 21, 23
[423] http://news.bbc.co.uk/1/hi/england/2410135.stm
[424] Tynemouth 1962a: 52
[425] *The Times* 3 Jul 1956, 24 Oct 1960
[426] *Gateshead Times* 5 Dec 1947
[427] Anon 1949: 16-19
[428] Stephenson Undated CD B
[429] *The Times* 4 Feb 1952
[430] Lloyd 1952a: 106, 116-17

[431] Lloyd 1952b: [7, endnote]
[432] *The Times* 7, 9 May 1955, 10, 28 Jan, 11 Mar 1957
[433] *Gateshead Post* 5 Sep 1958, 5 Jun 1960
[434] I owe this point to Ray Stephenson
[435] Anon 1959: 25-7
[436] Menzies 1899: 3-4, 6-7, 11
[437] *Newcastle Evening Chronicle* 23 Oct 1959
[438] *Gateshead Post* 5 Jun, 25 Nov 1960, 8 Jun 1962
[439] Walton Undated
[440] Gale 1970: 46
[441] *Gateshead Post* 8 Jun 1962
[442] Miles 1962
[443] *Sunderland Echo* 19 May 1962
[444] *Evening Chronicle* 30 May 1962
[445] Tynemouth 1962a: 5, 7, 23, 25, 27, 30, 33, 37, 41, 43, 50, 70
[446] *Gateshead Post* 8 Jun 1962
[447] Gale 1970: 56
[448] *Gateshead Post* 8 Jun 1962
[449] *The Journal* 8 Jun 1962
[450] Tynemouth 1962b
[451] *The Times* 11 Jun 1962
[452] **www.sclews.me.uk/m-taylor1.html**
[453] **www.benchtheatre.org.uk/plays80s/good.php**
[454] **www.sclews.me.uk/m-taylor1.html**
[455] *Evening Chronicle* 16 Oct 1970
[456] *The Times* 2, 5, 10 Mar, 8 Jun, 21 Dec 1964
[457] Graham 1965: 39-41, 45-6
[458] *The Times* 20 Apr 1967
[459] Gale 1970: 3, 13, 25-7
[460] Graham 1970: 2-5, 38-40
[461] *Evening Chronicle* 16 Oct 1970
[462] Tyne and Wear Archives 1845/DBC 364
[463] Newcastle Library
[464] *The Times* 1, 26 Jan 1971
[465] Harker 1973
[466] Manders 1973: 329-30
[467] *The Journal* 21 Mar 1974
[468] *The Times* 7 May 1977
[469] Lloyd 1978: 313
[470] *Gateshead Post* 19 Jan 1978
[471] *The Times* 24 Dec 1979

[472] http://news.bbc.co.uk/1/hi/england/2410135.stm
[473] www.asaplive.com/archive
[474] Gregson 2004
[475] http://en.wikipedia.org/wiki/Blaydon_Races
[476] Watson 2005
[477] www.twmuseums.org.uk/schools/tpl/uploads/BlaydonRaces—-Learning-Pack.pdf
[478] www.tomorrowshistory.com/projects/PF0100040001/George%20Ridley.htm
[479] *The Journal* 18 Mar 2011
[480] www.youtube.com/watch?v=84jwrWMp5js
[481] www.youtube.com/watch?v=Oq75BkicRZk
[482] Anon 2010
[483] *The Journal* 18 Mar 2011
[484] *Evening Chronicle* 17 Mar 2011
[485] *The Journal* 18 Mar 2011
[486] *Evening Chronicle* 18 Mar 2011, 22 Mar 2012

Sources

Adams, William Edwin (1903), *Memoirs of a Social Atom* (London: Hutchinson).

Allan, Maurice (1970-1972), correspondence, Author's collection.

Allan, Thomas, Allan Papers, Newcastle Library.

Allan, Thomas, ed. ([? 1862]), *Tyneside Songs*. Second Edition (Newcastle: Allan).

Allan, Thomas, ed. ([? 1864]), *Tyneside Songs*. Third Edition (Newcastle: Allan).

Allan, Thomas, ed. ([? 1865]), *A Choice Collection of Tyneside Songs* (Newcastle: Allan).

Allan, Thomas, ed. (1872), *A Choice Collection of Tyneside Songs* (Newcastle: Allan).

Allan, Thomas, ed. (1873), *A Choice Collection of Tyneside Songs* (Newcastle: Allan).

Allan, Thomas, ed. (1874), *A Choice Collection of Tyneside Songs* (Newcastle: Allan).

Allan, Thomas, ed. (1891), *Allan's Illustrated Edition of Tyneside Songs and Readings* (Newcastle: Allan).

Allen, Joan (2007), *Joseph Cowen* (Monmouth: Merlin).

Anon (Undated), *The Eclipse Self-Instructor for 5 string banjo* ([USA]).

Anon (1866), *Canteen songster: a collection of the most popular songs of the day, comprising Sentimental, Comic, Negro, Irish, National, Patriotic, Social, Convivial, and Pathetic Songs, Ballads, and Melodies* (Philadelphia: Simpson).

Anon (1891), 'Plague and Cholera in the North', *Monthly Chronicle* (Newcastle: Scott), 553-5.

Anon (1949), *Lingford's High Level Tyneside Song Book* (Bishop Auckland: Lingford).

Anon ([1959]), *Selection of Songs and Ballads of Northern England* (Newcastle: Allan).

Anon ([2010]), 'Blaydon Races' (Gateshead: Gateshead Council).

Anon (undated), 'Cuckoo Jack', 'Old Newcastle ... Music Hall, Circus, and Theatre', Newcastle Library

Barker, Kathleen (1983), 'The performing arts in Newcastle upon Tyne, 1840-70', in John Walton & James Walvin, eds, *Leisure in Britain*

1780-1939 (Manchester: Manchester University Press), 53-70.

Bell, David, & Edwin Patterson (1969), *Characters of old Tyneside* (Newcastle: Oriel Press).

Bennett, Anthony (1986), 'Music in the Halls', in J.S. Bratton, ed., *Music Hall. Performance and Style* (Milton Keynes: Open University Press, 1986), 1-22.

Burt, Thomas (1924), *An Autobiography* (London: T. Fisher Unwin).

Catcheside-Warrington, Charles Ernest, ed. (1911) *Tyneside Songs*, I (Newcastle: Windows).

Catcheside-Warrington, Charles Ernest, ed. (1912) *Tyneside Songs*, II (Newcastle: Windows).

Catcheside-Warrington, Charles Ernest, ed. (1913) *Tyneside Songs*, III (Newcastle: Windows).

Catcheside-Warrington, Charles Ernest, ed. (1924) *Tyneside Songs*, IV (Newcastle: Windows).

Catcheside-Warrington, Charles Ernest, ed. (1927) *Tyneside Songs*, I, (Newcastle: Windows).

Catcheside-Warrington, Charles Ernest, ed. (1929a) *Tyneside Songs*, II (Newcastle: Windows).

Catcheside-Warrington, Charles Ernest, ed. (1929b) *Tyneside Songs*, III (Newcastle: Windows).

Catcheside-Warrington, Charles Ernest, ed. (1929c) *Tyneside Songs*, IV (Newcastle: Windows).

Challinor, Raymond, & Brian Ripley (1968), *The Miners' Association* (London: Lawrence & Wishart)

Christie, John (1864), *Christie's new plan of Newcastle upon Tyne and Gateshead* (Newcastle: Christie).

Clarke, Joseph ([1979]), *Power on Land & Sea* (Newcastle: Hawthorn Leslie).

Cooter, Roger (2005), *When Paddy Met Geordie* (Sunderland: University of Sunderland Press).

Corvan, Edward ([? 1854), *Corvan's Song Book. 3.* (Newcastle: Walker). [Tyne & Wear Archives 1845/DBC/349]

Dixon, Graham, ed. (1987), *The Lads Like Beer. The Fiddle Music of James Hill* (Pathhead: Random).

Fane, Billy ([1985]), *A Life of Ridley* (Newcastle: *Evening Chronicle*).

French, David (2005), *Military Identities* (Oxford: Oxford University Press).

Fynes, Richard (1873), *The Miners of Northumberland and Durham* (Sunderland: Summerbell).

Gale, Joan (1970), *The Blaydon Races* (Newcastle: Oriel Press).

Gammon, Vic (2008), *Desire, Drink and Death in English Folk and Vernacular Song, 1600-1900* (Aldershot: Ashgate).

Gammon, Vic (2012) 'Blaydon Races', **www.tynefolk.co.uk/folk-articles.php**

Graham, Frank, ed. (1965), *Tyneside Songs* (Newcastle: Graham).

Graham, Frank, ed. (1970), *Tyneside Songster* (Newcastle: Graham).

Greenwell, George (1888) *A Glossary of Terms used in the Coal Trade.* (London: Beose).

Gregson, Keith (2004), 'Ridley, George [Geordie]', *Oxford Dictionary of National Biography* (Oxford: Oxford University Press).

Hall, Marshall (1996), 'The Painter of Blaydon Races', *The Northumbrian*, Number 12 (Winter 1996), 31-3.

Harker, Dave (1972), 'Thomas Allan and "Tyneside Song"', *Allan's Illustrated Edition of Tyneside Songs* (Newcastle: Frank Graham), iii-xxix.

Harker, David (1973), *George Ridley, Gateshead Poet and Vocalist* (Newcastle: Graham).

Harker, Dave, ed. (1985), *Songs from the Manuscript Collection of John Bell* (Durham: Surtees Society).

Harker, Dave (1986), 'Joe Wilson: "comic dialectical singer" or class traitor? ', in J.S. Bratton, ed., *Music Hall: Performance and Style* (Milton Keynes: Open University Press, 1986), 111-130.

Harker, Dave, ed. (1999), *Songs and Verse of the North East Pitmen, c.1780-1844* (Durham: Surtees Society).

Harrison, Rowland ([? 1872]), *Rowland Harrison's Tyneside Songs* ([?Newcastle]: [? Allan]).

Heslop, Richard Oliver (1892), *Northumberland Words* (London: English Dialect Society).

Heslop, Richard Oliver ['Harry Haldane'] (1896), *A Bibliographical List of Works Illustrative of the Dialect of Northumberland* (London: English Dialect Society).

Hume, Joseph, and others (1854), *Cholera Inquiry Commission* (London: Eyre & Spottiswoode).

Hunt, Christopher (1975), *The Book Trade in Northumberland and Durham to 1860* (Newcastle: Thorne).

Hutchinson, Joseph (1972), correspondence, Author's collection.

Jensen, Richard (2002) '"No Irish Need Apply": A Myth of Victimization', *Journal of Social History*, Volume 36, Number 2 (Winter 2002), 405-429.

Lewis, Samuel (1835), *A Topographical Dictionary of England*, (London: Lewis).

Lloyd, Albert Lancaster, ed. (1952a), *Coaldust Ballads* (London: Workers' Music Association).

Lloyd, Albert Lancaster, ed. (1952b), *Come All Ye Bold Miners* (London: Lawrence & Wishart).

Lloyd, Albert Lancaster, ed. (1978), *Come All Ye Bold Miners* (London: Lawrence & Wishart).

Mackenzie, Eneas (1827), *A Descriptive and Historical Account of the Town and County of Newcastle upon Tyne* (Newcastle: Mackenzie & Dent).

Manders, Frank (1973), *A History of Gateshead* (Gateshead: Gateshead Corporation).

Menzies, Thomas (1899), *Life of Joseph Hunter* (Newcastle: Bowes).

Miles, G.A. (1962), Letter to Clarence Watson, Gateshead Libraries.

Milne, Maurice (1971), *Newspapers of Northumberland and Durham* (Newcastle: Graham).

Morgan Alan (2007), *Victorian Panorama* (Newcastle: Tyne Bridge Publishing).

Nicholson, Joseph (1890), 'Cuckoo Jack', *Monthly Chronicle* (Newcastle: Scott), 110-14

Oliver, Thomas (1830), *Plan of Newcastle upon Tyne and the Borough of Gateshead* (Newcastle: Oliver)

Oliver, Thomas (1851), *Plan of Newcastle upon Tyne and Gateshead* (Newcastle: Oliver)

Reed, Archibald (1903), *Bruce's School* (Newcastle: Scott).

[Rewcastle, James] (1854), *Newcastle as It Is* (Newcastle: Barkas).

Ridley, George ([1862]), *George Ridley's Local Song Book* (Newcastle: Allan).

Ridley, George ([1863]), *George Ridley's New Local Song Book* (Newcastle: Allan).

Robson, Joseph Philip, ed. ([1849]), *Songs of the Bards of the Tyne* (Newcastle: France).

Robson, Joseph Philip (1854), *The Life and Adventures of Billy Purvis*. Third Edition (Newcastle: Christie).

Robson, Joseph Philip (1870), *The Autobiography of Joseph Philip Robson* (Newcastle: Chater).

Simpson, David (1998), 'Burning Questions', *Northern Echo*, 28 December 1998.

Stephenson, Ray (1981), 'Who's Who', *Northumbriana*, Number 22 (Spring 1981), 21-2.

Stephenson, Ray (1983), 'The Mystery of Eric Foster', *Northumbriana*, Number 27 (Summer 1983), 45-6.

Stephenson, Ray (1999]) *A Slice of Geordie Heritage* (Newcastle: Stephenson).

Stephenson, Ray (Undated CD A) *Legends Of The Lambton Worm And Blaydon Races. Original Tyneside dialect recordings 1909-1951* (Newcastle: Stephenson).

Stephenson, Ray (Undated CD B) *Legends of the Lambton Worm and the Blaydon Races. Original Tyneside dialect recordings 1909-1951* (Newcastle: Stephenson).

Tilly, Ray (2010) *Tommy Armstrong. The Pitman Poet* (Newcastle: Summerhill Books).

Todd, Nigel (1991), *The Militant Democracy* (Whitley Bay: Bewick Press).

Tynemouth, William (1962a), *Blaydon Races* (Newcastle: Newcastle City Libraries.)

Tynemouth, William (1962b), 'The Ninth of June', *Civic News*, Number 31, 9 June 1962 (Newcastle: Newcastle Corporation).

Walton, Clarence (Undated), 'Gateshead Personalities' [Cuttings, Gateshead Libraries.]

Watson, Elsdon, ed. ([2005]), *The Blaydon Races Heritage Trail 9th June 1862* (NP: Blaydon Races Festival Committee).

Wilson, Joe ([1873]), *Tyneside Songs, Ballads and Drolleries* (Newcastle: Allan).

Wilson, Joe ([1874]), *Temperance Songs, Readings, and Recitations, in the Tyneside Dialect, Comic and Sentimental* (Newcastle: Allan).

Wilson, Joe ([1890]), *Tyneside Songs and Drolleries. Readings and Temperance Songs* (Newcastle: Allan).

Discography

Early recordings are from Ray Stephenson's *A Slice of Geordie Heritage* - which is available from sedumray@talktalk.net - and Ray has put several on Stephenson Undated A and B. The later data is the work of Helen Mawson. (R) indicates a reissue.

Blaydon Races

c1908	J.C. Scatter	10 inch disc	Jumbo 208
1909	J.C. Scatter	Edison cylinder	Edison 13936
1911	C.E. Catcheside Warrington	78rpm disc	Zonophone 738
1913	J.C. Scatter	80rpm disc	Ariel Grand 1913 (R)
c1928	Jamieson Dodds	78rpm disc	Parlophone E3595
1929	Oxford Galleries Dance Band ('Blaydon Races One Step')	78rpm disc	Regal G9265
1929	Dewey Gibson	78rpm disc	Dominion A128
1929	J.C. Scatter	78rpm disc	Imperial 2149
1929	Catcheside E. Warrington	78rpm disc	Zonophone 5379
1929	St. Hilda's Colliery Band	78rpm disc	Regal G9423
1931	Catcheside Warrington	78rpm disc	Edison Bell 5368
1937	Jamieson Dodds	78rpm disc	Parlophone F683 (R)
1951	William Robinson	78 rpm disc	Manor M513
c1953	Five Smith Brothers	78rpm disc	EMI F2342
?	Five Smith Brothers	7 inch EP	Parlophone GEP8667 (R)
1957	Owen Brannigan	7 inch EP	HMV 7EP7050
1963	Owen Brannigan	12 inch LP	Delyse DS6069
1967	Owen Brannigan	12 inch LP	EMI CSD3639
1970	Sunderland Youth International Concert Band (instrumental)	12 inch LP	MWM1001s
1970	Michael Hunt	12 inch LP	Decca ECS2037
1970	High Level Ranters	12 inch LP	Trailer LER2020
1971	Owen Brannigan	12 inch LP	Decca 461 5492
1973	Owen Brannigan	12 inch LP	MWM1007 (R)
1975	Owen Brannigan	12 inch LP	MWM EC001
1979	Five Smith Brothers	12 inch LP	MWM1020 (R)
1972	Owen Brannigan	12 inch LP	Delyse ECS2105 (R)
1982	Alan Price	12 inch LP	MWMSP1
1983	Owen Brannigan	12 inch LP	MWMSP2
1984	Alan Price	12 inch LP	MWMSP3 (R)

1985	Billy Fane	12 inch LP	MWMSP6
1987	Thomas Allen & Sheila Armstrong	12 inch LP	MWMSP9
1987	Thomas Allen & Sheila Armstrong	Cassette	MWMCSP9
1987	Thomas Allen & Sheila Armstrong	CD	MWMCDSP9
1993	Thomas Allen	VHS video	SONV1001
1993	Thomas Allen	CD	MWMCDSP12
1993	Thomas Allen	Cassette	MWMCSP12
1995	Sunderland Youth International Concert Band (instrumental)	CD	MWMCDSP18 (R)
1987	Owen Brannigan	CD	Decca 461 5492 (R)
1998	Owen Brannigan ('Brown Ale Song')	CD	MWMCDSP22
1998	Graeme Danby	CD	MWMCDSP22
1998	Lemington Male Voice Choir	CD	LMVCCD2
2000	Billy Fane	CD	MWMCDSP25 (R)
2001	Owen Brannigan	CD	Decca 467 782-2
2002	Thomas Allen & Sheila Armstrong	CD	MWMCDSP44
2003	Roly Veitch	CD	RVCD1
2004	Alan Clarke (instrumental)	DVD	MWMDVD1010
2007	Houghton Weavers	CD	Townsend
2008	Graeme Danby	DVD	MWMDVD84
2008	Thomas Allen & Sheila Armstrong	CD	MWMSP86 (R)
2008	Thomas Allen	CD	MWMCDSP87 (R)
2008	Thomas Allen	DVD	MWMDVD88 (R)
2009	Houghton Weavers	MP3	Townsend
2009	Tim Healy, Jimmy Nail, Kevin Whately	DVD	MWMDVD98
2012	Tim Healy, Jimmy Nail, Kevin Whately	DVD	MWMDVD78

The Bobby Cure

2002	Johnny Handle	CD	MWMCD43

Cushie Butterfield

1911	Ernest Warrington	78rpm disc	Zonophone 738
c1928	Jamieson Dodds	78rpm disc	Parlophone E3595
1929	Catcheside E. Warrington	78rpm disc	Zonophone 5495
1929	Catcheside E. Warrington	78rpm disc	Regal 5495
1931	Catcheside Warrington	78rpm disc	Edison Bell 5392
1937	Jamieson Dodds	78rpm disc	Parlophone F683 (R)
1951	William Robinson	78rpm disc	Manor M513
c1953	Five Smith Brothers	78rpm disc	Parlophone R3725
1960	Owen Brannigan	7 inch EP	HMV 7EG8551

1963	Owen Brannigan	12 inch LP	Delyse DS6069
1967	Owen Brannigan	12 inch LP	EMI CSD3639
1967	Michael Hunt	12 inch LP	Decca LK4902
1970	Michael Hunt	12 inch LP	Decca ECS2307(R)
1970	High Level Ranters	12 inch LP	Trailer LER2020
1971	Owen Brannigan	12 inch LP	Decca 461 5492
1972	Owen Brannigan	12 inch LP	Delyse ECS2105 (R)
1972	The Shiremoor Marras	12 inch LP	MWM1005s
1973	Owen Brannigan	12 inch LP	MWM1007(R)
1975	Alex Glasgow	12 inch LP	MWM1011
1975	High Level Ranters	12 inch LP	MWM EC001 (R)
1979	Five Smith Brothers	12 inch LP	MWM1020 (R)
1982	Alan Price	12 inch LP	MWMSP1
1984	Alan Price	12 inch LP	MWMSP3 (R)
1985	Billy Fane	12 inch LP	MWMSP6
1993	Thomas Allen	CD	MWMCDSP12
1994	Thomas Allen	VHS video	SONV1001
1995	The Shiremoor Marras	CD	MWMCDSP18 (R)
1997	Alex Glasgow	CD	MWMCDSP21 (R)
1997	Owen Brannigan	CD	Decca 461 5492
1998	Graeme Danby	CD	MWMCDSP22
1998	Owen Brannigan ('Brown Ale Song')	CD	MWMCDSP22
2000	Billy Fane	CD	MWMCDSP25 (R)
2001	Denis Weatherley	CD	MWMCDSP27
2002	Thomas Allen	CD	MWMCDSP43
2002	Thomas Allen	CD	MWMCDSP51 (R)
2003	Roly Veitch	CD	RVCD1
2007	Houghton Weavers	CD	Townsend Records
2008	Thomas Allen & Sheila Armstrong	CD	MWMSP87 (R)
2008	Thomas Allen	CD	MWMSP87 (R)
2008	Thomas Allen	DVD	MWMDVD88 (R)
2009	Houghton Weavers	MP3	Townsend Records

Joey Jones

2010	Jim Mageean	CD	BITCD316

Shields Lass for Me

1985	Billy Fane	12 inch LP	MWMSP6
2000	Billy Fane	CD	MWMCDSP25 (R)
2002	Billy Fane	CD	MWMCD35 (R)

Song and Tune Index

Aa hope ye'll be kind te me Dowter 125
After the Ball 121
Annie Laurie 83
Artful Dodger 83
Ask for Nothing More 84
Aud (Awd) Bob Ridley 49, 83
Aw'm (I'm) Afloat 92
Bay of Biscay 71
Ben Bolt 84
Billy Nutts 39
Billy Pattison 83
Black Cure 49
Blaydon Keelman, The 50, 80-1, 103
Blaydon Races 4-6, 63-6, 68, 82, 89, 95, 99, 109-12, 116, 123, 125-7, 129, 131-50
Blind Willie's Deeth 89-90
Blue Star Song, The 135-6
Bobbing Joan 70
Bobby Cure, The 41-2, 80-1, 90, 107, 112, 146
Brighton 64, 66
Broken-Hearted Keelman (Cushie Butterfield)
Bullerwell and Summer's Race 60-1, 80-1, 103
Cabman, The 54-5, 80-1
Cappy 58
Chambers 87-90, 112
[Clasper and Drewitt?] 63
Cliffs of old Tynemouth, The 125, 134
Coal Black Rose 48
Come, come with me to the Old Kirkyard 28
Cottage by the Sea 83
Courting in the Kitchen 70
Cullercoats Fishlass, The 147-8
Cushey (Cushie) Butterfield 6, 91-2, 95, 97, 102, 124-6, 129, 131-6, 138-42, 144-8
Dada's Baby Boy 121
Dixey's Land 50
Doran's Ass 83
Gallowgate Lad, The 125

Gee Ho Dobbin 58
Gentle Annie 83
Geordie Haad the Bairn 125-6, 134
God Save the Queen 84
God speed ye all ye hopeful band 28
Hail Smiling Morn 28
Hamlet 70
Happiest Man Alive, The 56
Harry Clasper and His Testimonial 58-9
Hey John Barleycorn 72
Highland Mary 37
Hogg and Foster's Race 53, 80-1
Joey Jones 38, 51, 80-1, 111
John Barleycorn 82, 84
Johnny Luik-Up 39-42, 80-2, 90, 105-6, 112
John Spencer (All Aboard for a Penny) 71-2, 80-2, 92, 112
Jolly Waggoner 83
Keel Row, The 125, 129, 141
Keep Yor Feet Still, Geordy Hinney 125, 127, 134
Kiss Me Quick and Go 53
Lambton Worm, The 134
Larry O'Gaff 37
Last Neet 125
Last Rose of Summer 84
Limerick Races 83
Low Back'd Car 83
Magistrates at the Concert, The 62
Mally Dunn 125
Minnie Clyde 83
Mrs Bond 54
My Old Dutch 121
My own my Guiding Star 84
Nancy Till 83
Nelly Bly 84
Nelly Grey 83
New Blaydon Races 142
Newcastle Celebrities (Eccentrics) 52, 80-1
Newcastle Props, The 89-90
No Irish Need Apply 84
Nothing More 52

Old Arm Chair 84
Old Bog Hole 84
Old Folks at Home 28
Old Hog or None 56
Ole King Cole 84
On the Road to Brighton 67
Paddy Fagan 65, 110
Pat Murphy 84
Pat of Mullingar 38, 83
Pawnshop Bleezin', The 125
Perfect Cure, The 41, 83
Peter Grey 83
Phoebe Morel, or I Had a Dream 48
Postman's Knock 84
Pretty Polly Perkins 91, 133
Ragged Coat 84
Rakes of Stoney Batter 70
Rifleman (Riflemen), The 48-9, 51, 80-2, 103
Robin Grey 83
Rosalie the Prairie Flower 83
Sally Come Up 39
Sheels Lass for Me, The 83-4, 89, 112, 136, 144, 146
Slaves Dream, The 48
Snooks the Artist 39
So early in the Morning 84
Spider and the Fly, The 54
Stephenson Monument, The 72-4, 82, 89, 112
Tanfield Brake, The 99
Teasdale Wilson, the City Champion 56-7, 82, 89, 102-3
There is a Flower that Bloometh 84
Time Gun, The 91, 95
'Tis hard to give the Hand 83
Wait for the Waggon 83
What's a' the Steer, Kimmer 84
Whole Hog or None, The 56, 63, 83, 87
Widow Machree 83
Will you come to the Bower 54
Young Man from the Country 60, 83-4
Young Recruit 48

Name Index

Abbott, John 49
Airey, Doctor 20-1
Alabama Minstrels 68
Alberto, Signor Carlo 25
Aldcroft, Tom 38
Alderson & Brentnall 139
Aleck (flautist) 49
Allan Alice (McDougal) 76, 79
Allan, Alice (William senior's daughter) 111
Allan, Ann (Ralph senior's wife) 79, 100, 111, 115
Allan, Annie senior (Thomas senior's wife) 99-100, 106, 111, 116, 127
Allan, Annie junior (Thomas senior's daughter) 111
Allan, Edward 106, 111, 113, 116, 127
Allan, Elizabeth senior (Thomas senior's sister) 76, 79, 106, 111
Allan, Elizabeth junior (Thomas senior's daughter) 111, 116
Allan, Elizabeth (George's wife) 107
Allan, Ethel 100, 106, 115
Allan, Florence (Flora) Alice 111, 116
Allan, George 76, 79, 96, 104-7, 109-12, 125-6, 132, 135, 137, 141, 149
Allan, George William 106, 111, 113-14, 116, 127
Allan, Isabella 100, 106, 115
Allan, James 79, 100, 106
Allan, Kate 107
Allan, Mary Elizabeth 106, 111
Allan, Maurice 76, 142
Allan, Nicholas 76, 79, 107-8
Allan, Nora J. 111
Allan, Ralph (Thomas senior's father) 76-7, 79
Allan, Ralph junior 85, 95-7, 100-1, 103-4, 106, 108-9, 111-13, 115-16
Allan, Ralph (Ralph junior's son) 100, 106, 108-9, 113, 116
Allan, Robert 76, 79
Allan, Thomas senior 6, 59, 61, 76-82, 84-5, 89-93, 95-107, 109-13, 125-6, 132, 135, 137, 141, 149
Allan, Thomas junior 100, 106, 111
Allan, William senior 76, 79, 106, 111-15
Allan, William junior 106, 111
Allen, Thomas 144, 146
Allhusson, Christian 48
Anderson, Henry 32
Animals, The 144
Armstrong, Annie (Annie Allan senior)
Armstrong, Edward 99
Armstrong, Elizabeth 100, 106, 111, 116, 126
Armstrong, Sheila 144, 146
Armstrong, Tommy 99
Armstrong, Sir William 48-50, 52, 64, 110
Arthey, Vin 6, 113
Bache, Emily (Stanley)
Baker, Paul 6
Balmbra, John 6, 23-31, 34-5, 38, 47-8, 63-4, 74, 93, 99, 110, 132, 138, 141, 148-50
Balmbra, Isabella 27, 29, 34-6, 47-8, 99
Barras, Percival Frederick 129
Beal (printer) 81
Belley (runner) 53
Bennehan, Sophia (Catcheside)
Bennett, Reverend William 94
Bennette, S. (comedian) 24
Benson, George 109-10
Bewick, Thomas 27
Bladey, Conrad 66
Boucicault, Dion 98
Boutland, Thomas 24, 30
Boyd, Barry 144
Braban, Ann 28
Brannigan, Owen 135-42, 145-6, 148
British Motor Corporation Concert Band 140, 142, 145
Brothers Handford (Joe and Tom)
Brown, Ann 107
Brown, Jackey 65, 110
Brown, Robert 107
Brown Ale Brass Band 146
Bruce, John Collingwood 126
Buckley, G. Swaine 39
Bullerwell, Bob 60-1
Burgess, Roger 140
Butterfield, 'Cushey' 115
Calder, Maggie 124
Caldwell, John 15
Campbell, Paul 149
Carmichael, John William 12
Carr, Tommy 48
Carter, President Jimmy 143
Catcheside, Ada (Livermore) 119
Catcheside, Annie Wardlaw K. 118-19, 123
Catcheside, Bertha 119, 123-4
Catcheside, Charles Ernest 6, 118-33
'Catcheside, E.' (Charles Ernest Catcheside)

Catcheside, George 118
Catcheside, Louisa Mary 118
Catcheside, Mary 118
Catcheside, Mona 119, 123-4
Catcheside, Robert 118-19
Catcheside, Robert Marium 118-19, 122
Catcheside, Sophia 119
'Catcheside-Warrington, C.E.' (Charles Ernest Catcheside)
Catcheside-Warrington, Helen Edith (Warrington)
'Catchy' (Charles Ernest Catcheside)
Chambers, Robert ('Bob') 49-52, 59, 87-8, 90, 93
Chandler, Chas 144
Chevalier, Albert 121
Christie, John 45
Christy Minstrels 57, 62
Clarke, Alan 147
Clasper Harry 49-52, 58-9, 62-3
Clasper, John ('Jack') 49-52, 63
Clasper, Dickey 57
Clifton, Harry 91
Clinton (bandleader) 48
'Coffee Johnny '(Oliver) 49-50, 65, 99, 110, 114-16
Collins, Margaret 35
Collis, Miss (singer) 26
Conolly, Patrick 29
Consett Citizens' Choir 140
Conway, Terry 7
Cooper (rower) 88
Corvan, Ned 39, 84-5, 95-6, 101, 106, 147
Cosgrove, Isabella 123-4
Cosgrove, James ('Scatter') 6, 123-4, 129, 131
Court Minstrels 119
Coutts, Charlie 49
Cowell, Samuel 70
Cowen, Jane (Thompson) 33
Cowen, John 32
Cowen, Joseph senior 32, 36, 50, 96, 98, 104
Cowen, Joseph junior 32-4, 36, 44, 46, 55, 84-5, 88, 98-9, 104, 108-9, 114
Cowen, Mary (Newbiggin) 32
Cowen, Mary (Newton) 32
Cowen, Mary (Forster)
Crawshay, George 19, 94
Crony, Kate 124
Crookhall Colliery Band 138
Crowley's ironworks 32, 136
'Cuckoo Jack' (John Wilson) 51-2
Cuthbertson, T. Leslie 4, 136
Daggett, Steve 149
Danby, Graeme 146, 148
Davidson, J. (runner) 103
Davies, Rees 107
Davis, Joseph 79-81
Decca 141
Derbyshire, James Watson 86-7
Desborough, Juliet 62
Deucher, James 116
Dire Straits 147
Dobrowski (pianist) 121
Dobson, Scott 140
Dodds, Jamieson 129, 131
Dodds, Jimmy 53
Dodds, Mary (Catcheside)
Dombie Brothers 140
Donald, Adam Elphinstone 30-1, 37, 97, 99
Donald, James 30
Donald, Janet 30
Donald, John 30
Donald, Margaret Forster (Jamieson) 30, 99
Doyle (jockey) 38
Drewitt, George 63
Easton, Thomas 12, 14
Easthope, Charles 24, 26-7, 29, 74
Easthope, Margaret 27, 74
Ecclestone, William 116-17
Edison, Thomas 123
Edison Bell Consolidated Phonograph Company 123
'Elfin' (Hawkes) 55-6, 62, 68, 94
Eltringham, Elizabeth 35
Emery, Robert 97, 101
EMI 140, 142-3
Emmett, Daniel Decatur 50
Engels, Friedrich 33, 108
English National Opera 146
English, Isabella (Wilson)
Everson (rower) 88
Fane, Billy 66, 103, 144, 146
Felling Male Voice Choir 137
Fentiman, Anni 7
Fife, Sir John 48
Five Smith Brothers 133, 138, 143
Fobert (horse owner) 38
Fordyce, Thomas 96-7, 100, 105
Forester, Alec 135

Forster, Anthony 32
Forster, Mary 32
Forster, Joseph ('Tout') 52-3
Forster, Thomas 98
'Foster, Eric' (Charles Ernest Catcheside)
Foster, Stephen 28
French, Jane (Ridley)
Gaitskell, Hugh 139
Gale, Ann 124
Gale, Jane (Windows)
Gale, Joan 140-1
Gammon, Vic 6-7, 48, 54, 56, 58, 66, 70, 72, 133
Garibaldi, Giuseppe 33-4, 55
Gibb, Doctor C.J. 65, 110
Gibbon, Mary Ann 28
Gibbons, Hannah 111
Gibson, Dewey 129
Gilbert, Vicki 6
Gilchrist, Robert 101
Gill, Madame C.C. 24
Gilley (runner) 53
Gillings, Dave 119-23
Glasgow, Alex 142
Gowdy, Louisa Mary (Catcheside)
Graham, Benny 7
Graham, Frank 6, 139, 141-2
Grahamsley (farmer) 20
Grainger, Richard 52
Gramophone Company 124
Green, Richard 87
Gregson, Keith 7, 147, 149
Gregson, Thomas 79-80
Hadlow (horse owner) 38
Hair, Thomas Harrison 14
Hall, Marky 53
Handford, Joe 47-9
Handford, Tom 47-9, 92-3
Handford, Mrs 48
Handle, Johnny 7, 147
Hardwick, Charlie 149
Hardy, Stewart 7
Harker, Dave 142
Harris, Helen Edith (Warrington)
Harrison, Rowland 101
Harvey, William 17
Haslam, Dave 144-6
Hawkes, Sidney Milnes ('Elfin')
Hawks, George 20, 49, 94
Hawthorn, Robert & William 49, 77-8
Healy, Tim 149
Hedley, Thomas L. 111
Helliwell, Clifton 146
Henderson, Fanny (Stephenson)
Henderson, Hilda 137, 143
'Henwife Jack' 52
Herman, Simon 25
Heslop, Richard Oliver 111, 126
Hetherington (?), Elizabeth Jane 116
Hetherington, Janet Ann (Ridley)
Hexham, Bishop of 130
Higgins, John 39-41, 81, 102-3, 105-6, 112
High Level Ranters 141-2
Hill, Jimmy 37
Hodge, James 49
Hogg, Joseph 52-3, 102
Hogg, Neddy 53
Hook, Theodore 70
'Hopey' (rower) 56
Houghton Weavers 148
House, George 140
Howitt, Mary 54
Hume, W.E. (librarian) 137
Hunt, Michael 140-1
Hunter, Joseph 136
Hutchinson, Joseph 142
Hyndman, Henry 108
Irving, Ken 147
Irving, William 114-16, 131, 147 -8
Jackson (horse owner) 38
Jamieson, Margaret Forster (Donald)
Jefferies, Peter 7, 94
'Johnny Luik-Up' (Higgins)
Jordinson, James 115
Kears, Robert 15
Kelly (rower) 88
Kossuth, Lajos 34
Kropotkin, Prince Peter 108
Laidlaw, Ray 149
Leatherland, Joe 140
Lindisfarne 141
Lingford & Son, Joseph 132
Lisle, William 77
Livermore, Ada (Catcheside)
Livermore, Horace 119
Livermore, Lechmere 119
Lloyd, Albert Lancaster 132-3, 143
Londonderry, Lord 13

Lough, John Graham 72
Low Fell Ladies Choir 140
Lush, Ernest 137
McDermott, G.H. (agent) 120
McDougal, Alice (Allan)
McGibbon, Annie Wardlaw K. (Catcheside)
McGibbon, James 118, 123
McGibbon, Jessie 123
McLean, Ronnie 139-40
Mackney, E.W. (composer) 39
Mageean, Jim 7
Manders, Frank 142
Martin, Francis 119
Marx, Karl 33, 108
Mason, Miss M. (dancer) 26
Matfen (rower) 56-7
Matheson, Duncan 16
Mawson, Brian 7, 125, 139-40, 142
Mawson, Helen 7, 125, 139
Mawson & Wareham (Music) 140, 142-9
Mawson, Swan & Morgan 116
Mazzini, Giuseppe 32-4, 55
Mellor (actor) 25
Menzies, Thomas 136
Miller (runner) 53
Mitchell, Billy 149
Mitford, William 101
Morrison (factory owner) 49
Mortimer, Harry 140
Moss, J. (singer) 68
Muir, Jimmy 129-30
Musical Mozarts 120-3
Nail, Jimmy 149
Napoleon III, Emperor Louis 34, 55, 108
Nelson, Peter 113-14
Neville, Mike 140
New Orleans Jazz Club 139
Newbiggin, Mary (Cowen)
Newcastle police band 138
Newton, Mary (Cowen senior)
Northern Sinfonia Orchestra 137, 144
Northumbrian Traditional Group 142
Norvel, Tom 53
Nunn, Bobby 78-9, 90, 127
Nuttall, J. (runner) 102
Ogilvie, John 29
Oliver, John ('Coffee Johnny')
Oliver, Thomas 10, 18
Oliver, William 90, 101
O'Neil, Denis 16
Oppenheimer Brothers 125
Orsini, Felice 34
Osborne (horse owner) 38
Oxford Galleries Dance Band 129
Oxwell, Annie 116
Paganini, Niccolo 26
Parker (omnibus owner) 63, 65
Paxton, W. & Co. 127
Pickford, Mary Ann 111
Philipson (runner) 53
Poole, John F. 84
Porter, John 11
Porter, Mary (Ridley)
Price, Alan 144
Pringle, David 20
Purvis, Billy 23-4, 41
Purvis, Blind Willie 90
Ramsay, T. (lyricist) 39
'Ranter' 52
Ravensworth, Lord 12
Reay, Jimmy 53
Reay, Samuel 127
Reed, Archibald 30
Reuben Brothers 136
Richardson, Catherine 111
Ridley, Barbara 11
Ridley, Benjamin (George's brother) 35, 99, 107, 111, 115-16, 127
Ridley, Benjamin (Stephenson senior's son) 107
Ridley, Benjamin (Young senior's son) 115-16
Ridley, Caroline 99, 107
Ridley, David (George's great-grandfather) 11
Ridley, David (George's brother) 17, 35-6, 99, 114
Ridley, Elena (Elleanor, Ellen) 35, 99, 107, 109
Ridley, Elizabeth (George's sister) 11, 17, 35, 108, 117
Ridley, Elizabeth (Matthew junior's wife) 99
Ridley, Elizabeth (Young senior's wife) 99, 107, 109, 116
Ridley, Elizabeth (John senior's daughter) 35, 99
Ridley, Elizabeth (Young senior's daughter) 100, 107
Ridley, Elizabeth Ann (John junior's wife) 117
Ridley, Esther senior (Robert junior's wife) 117
Ridley, Esther junior (Robert junior's daughter) 117
Ridley, Frances (George's mother) 11, 17, 35, 73-4, 93-4, 99, 105

Ridley, Frances (Benjamin senior's daughter) 111, 115-16
Ridley, Frances (Stephenson senior's daughter) 117
Ridley, George (songwriter) 4-6, 12-13, 15, 17, 20-2, 35-42, 47-75, 79-85, 87-9, 100-2, 106-7, 111-13, 117, 129, 132-43, 145, 147-8, 150
Ridley, George (Stephenson senior's son) 117
Ridley, Hannah 35, 99, 107, 117
Ridley, Hilda (Henderson)
Ridley, Isabella (Belle) (John senior's daughter) 107, 109
Ridley, Isabella (Young senior's daughter) 107, 109, 116
Ridley, Jack (Stephenson senior's grandson?) 137
Ridley, Jane 111, 115-16
Ridley, Janet Ann senior 100, 107, 116
Ridley, Janet Ann junior (Stephenson senior's daughter) 117
Ridley, Joan (Joann) 109, 115-16
Ridley, John (George's brother) 11, 17, 35, 99, 107, 109, 117, 127
Ridley, John junior (John senior's son) 117
Ridley, John (Benjamin senior's son) 111, 115-16
Ridley, John (Stephenson senior's son) 117, 137
Ridley, John George 117
Ridley, Joseph 116
Ridley, Margaret (John senior's wife) 117
Ridley, Margaret (Stephenson senior's daughter) 117
Ridley, Margaret Jane 117
Ridley, Mary (George's grandmother) 11
Ridley, Mary (George's sister) 20, 35, 100, 117
Ridley, Mary (John senior's daughter) 99, 107, 109, 117
Ridley, Mary (Young senior's daughter) 100, 107, 109, 116
Ridley, Matthew senior (George's father) 11-13, 17, 35, 99, 104, 115-16
Ridley, Matthew junior (George's brother) 12, 17, 36, 99, 107, 109, 116, 129
Ridley, Matthew (John senior's son) 117
Ridley, Richard (Stephenson senior's son) 117
Ridley, Richard (Stephenson senior's grandson) 136-7
Ridley, Robert senior (Stephenson senior's son) 117, 137
Ridley, Robert junior 117
Ridley, Sarah 117
Ridley, Sarah Jane 117
Ridley, Stephenson senior (Stephen, Joseph Stephenson, Joseph Stevenson) 5, 17, 35100, 102-3, 107-8, 116, 136-7, 143
Ridley, Stephenson junior (Stephenson senior's son) 117
Ridley, Susannah 117
Ridley, Thomas 111, 115-16
Ridley, Thomas Cooper 117
Ridley, William 15
Ridley, Young (George's grandfather) 11, 17
Ridley, Young senior (George's brother) 12, 17, 36, 99, 107-9, 113
Ridley, Young junior (Young senior's son) 100, 107, 109, 116
Ritchie, John 93
Robinson, Francis 117
Robinson, James 21
Robinson, William 132
Robson (contractor) 43
Robson, Sir Bobby 149
Robson, Eric 149
Robson, Joseph Philip 85, 97, 101
Rowan (runner) 53
Rowell, Henry 100
Royal Regiment of Fusiliers Band 149
Russell, Henry 54
Rutter, Christopher 77-8
Sahnow, Will 133-4
St. Hilda's Colliery Band 129
Sangar Brothers 43
Sanderson, Bob 49
'Scatter, J.C.' (Cosgrove)
Scott, Adam 71
Scott, Robert 99
Sessford, Eleanor 23
Sessford, John ('Jack') 23-8, 30, 74
Sessford, John junior 27
Sessford, Joseph 23
Sessford, Mary senior 27, 74
Sessford, Mary junior 27
Shakespeare, William 70, 88
Shanks, Tommy 54
Sharpe (horse owner) 38
'Sheldon, Ernest' (Robert Marium Catcheside)
Shield, John 101
Shiremoor Marras 142
Smedley, Ralph 140
Smith, Hugh 46
Spencer, John ('Jack') 68-72

Spiers, James H. 24-6, 29, 49
Stanley, Emilie 43, 84
Stanley, Frances 93
Stanley, George William 43-9, 51, 55-6, 58-9, 62, 68, 84, 86, 88-9, 93-8, 103, 105, 114
Stanley, Samuel 43
Stead, James Henry 41
Stephenson, Elizabeth 17, 35, 99
Stephenson, Fanny 73
Stephenson, Frances (Ridley)
Stephenson, George 72-5
Stephenson, Martha 35
Stephenson, Ray 7
Stephenson, Robert 49, 52, 73-4, 79, 89
Stephenson, Thomas 17, 35, 99
Stirling, T. (singer) 97
Stokoe, John 126
Storey, John 35, 45
Strother, Isabella C. 106
Summers (runner) 60-1
Sunderland Youth International Concert Band 140
Sydney, Alfred 119
Taylor, Cecil 139
Taylor, John 59
Thompson, Bobby 143
Thompson, Jane (Cowen)
Todd, Elizabeth 107
Tom, 'cock-eyed' 40
Trailer Records 141
Turnbull, Annie 124
Tute, J.T. (band leader) 86
Tynemouth, William 138
Usher, Launcelot & Robert 76
Vallance, Thomas 33
Victoria, Queen 45, 52, 72
Waitt, Mary Elizabeth 116
Wallsend Youth Theatre 141
Walton, Clarence 132-3
Wappat, Frank 146
Ward, J. (singer) 25
Ward, Tom 147
Wareham, Derek 140
Warrington, Annie (Catcheside)
Warrington, Bertha (Catcheside)
Warrington, Helen Winifred Edythe 123
Warrington, Mona (Catcheside)
'Warrington, Charles' (Charles Ernest Catcheside)
'Warrington, Charles E.' (Charles Ernest Catcheside)
'Warrington, Ernest' (Charles Ernest Catcheside)
Watson, Brian 7
Watson, James 104
Watson (horse trainer) 38
Weatherley, Denis 146
Week (schoolteacher) 32
Whately, Kevin 149
White (rower) 88
White (runner) 53
Wildbore, Geordy 53
Wilkelmind (servant) 115
Wilkes, Geraldine 140
Wilkinson, Arthur 135
William IV, King 20
Williams, William 16
Wilson, Isabella 100, 105-6
Wilson, John ('Cuckoo Jack')
Wilson, Joseph 81, 100, 103-9, 126-7
Wilson, Teasdale 56-7, 102
Windley, Mary 28
Windows, Fanny 124
Windows, Hedley 124
Windows, James Gale 6, 124-9, 139
Windows, Jane 124
Windows, Joseph 124
Windows, Maud 124, 129
Windows, Maurice James 124, 139
Winship, Edward 49-52
Wonfor, Geoff 144, 149
Wood, William K. 67
Woodmass, Harold 130
Yale Music Corporation 134
Young, Barbara (Ridley)
Young, Jonathan Lewis 120-1
Young (landlord) 71
Young (sculptor) 93
Younge, R.W. (impressario) 114